Examine Your Faith! provides answers to unanswered questions most people have that are preventing them from embracing and living life with confidence. If you are not confident about what you believe, *or what makes sense to believe*, this book will help you examine the popular faith claims of our day and discover life-giving truth. **Josh D. McDowell, Author and Speaker**

Pamela Christian's stated goal in her book *Examine Your Faith! Finding Truth in a World of Lies* is to help readers "realize the eternal importance of examining what you believe and why you believe it." After an initial evaluation of the interrelatedness of faith, knowledge, and truth, she approaches this task in a unique and compelling fashion. Rather than apply typical apologetic methods of argumentation, she uncritically lays out the main tenets of Christianity's major religious and secular competitors—and then challenges her readers to determine *for themselves* which worldview is best supported by objective facts. Religious skeptics, spiritual seekers, or those who simply want to examine their faith to determine its legitimacy cannot read this book without concluding that Christianity has no competitors. It alone is objectively true and meets human needs at their deepest emotional and spiritual levels. **Dan Story, MA, Christian Apologetics, Author and Teacher**

Pamela Christian has done something here that is very difficult to do. That is, she has written an engaging and personal, yet thoughtful and fact-filled book in Christian apologetics. This is a wonderful introduction to both world religions and the special case for Christ. And it is perfect for group studies at churches everywhere. **Craig J. Hazen, Ph.D., Founder and Director, Graduate Program in Christian Apologetics, Biola University, Author of *Five Sacred Crossings***

Pamela Christian has approached the finding of truth in a refreshing, challenging way, one that enables readers to use their own thought processes to arrive at a logical and satisfying conclusion. Whether you are still in that initial search for truth or simply wanting to strengthen your existing convictions, *Examine Your Faith! Finding Truth in a World of Lies* will help you reach your goal. **Kathi Macias, Author and Speaker**

Pamela Christian (the "Faith Doctor") has formulated the antidote to the postmodern malaise. Appealing to believers and nonbelievers alike, she advocates a robust review of the *what* and *why* of the major contestants vying for worldview supremacy. *Examine Your Faith! Finding Truth in a World of Lies* takes a bold and candid approach to exposing the flaws of non-Christian thinking, and demonstrates that only through faith in Jesus Christ can we adequately account for the universe, the human condition, and our desire for meaning and purpose. A real spiritual workout! **Stanley M. Tarbell, MA, Bible Teacher and Speaker**

Faith is one of the most written about yet misunderstood aspects of Christianity. But in *Examine Your Faith! Finding Truth in a World of Lies*, Pamela Christian takes us on a remarkable journey. Through her own story, she will help change the way the next generation understands what real faith means. If you've ever experienced doubt, then this is the book for you. You'll discover more confidence in your faith than you ever dreamed possible. **Kathleen Cooke, V.P. Cooke Pictures**

Faith is to our souls what a steering wheel is to a car. If it's working, we're pointed in the right direction. If it's not, we are in peril! Pamela Christian's *Examine Your Faith!* is a gift that helps clarify the direction of our souls. I recommend it for you and those you care about. **Ron Forseth, Vice President, Outreach, Inc.**

While struggling with a personal crisis, Pamela Christian was forced to examine her faith and why she believed what she believed. *Examine Your Faith!* recounts her journey of investigating the world's most influential religious systems and her quest to build a faith grounded in truth. Along the way, she educates, motivates, and inspires—concluding with a compelling case for why the best placed faith is a faith in Jesus Christ. This is the ideal book for anyone who is hungry for answers about life's most important questions. Truly a five-star book! **Britt Gillette, Author and Founder of End Times Bible Prophecy website**

EXAMINE YOUR FAITH!

FINDING TRUTH IN A WORLD OF LIES

Pamela Christian

The Faith Doctor with Your Rx for Life!

WestBow
PRESS
A DIVISION OF THOMAS NELSON

Examine Your Faith!
Finding Truth in a World of Lies

WestBow Press books may be ordered through booksellers or by contacting:
WestBow Press
A Division of Thomas Nelson
1663 Liberty Drive
Bloomington, IN 47403
www.westbowpress.com
1-(866) 928-1240

Published by:
Pamela Christian Ministries
18032 Lemon Dr. #C206, Yorba Linda, CA 92886
info@pamelachristianministries.com

ISBN: 978-1-4497-9919-9 (sc)
ISBN: 978-1-4497-9920-5 (hc)
ISBN: 978-1-4497-9918-2 (e)
Library of Congress Control Number: 2013911358

Printed in the United States of America.
WestBow Press rev. date: 8/13/2013

With profound gratitude, I prayerfully dedicate this book to the One who made finding truth possible for anyone and everyone who wants to find it.

Contents

Acknowledgments

Were it not for the unknown numbers of men, women, and children, throughout all time and history, who honestly sought to find truth then to help others find it, I would not know truth. Thanks to them, the truth was passed down to people who've influenced and shaped my life—family, friends and perfect strangers—who by word or deed, visible or unknown to me, have had an eternal impact on my life. I especially acknowledge the precious people of my church homes, Community Bible Study, and Christian media, along with personal friends and family as my "Truth Investors."

Since I have concluded that Christianity is the one faith that offers the best explanation for the meaning of life and hope for all creation, it was apparent that my addressing other religious beliefs could be suspect by the reader as biased. In an effort to avoid that and be as accurate as possible I sought respected men and women who were reared in the specific religions, asking them to review what I wrote for any needed correction. Particular gratitude is owed to Dan Story—a special mentor of mine. His expertise and encouragement challenged me to dig deeper to produce the quality work that was in my heart to do. Thanks also belong to Bonnie Compton Hanson and Dr. Melanie Brady for their reviews, and to my editor, Amanda Rooker, and her staff. Their contributions helped polish my work.

For all that I have gained from you who have gone before me and assisted me not only in writing this book but in life, my only reasonable response is to attempt to follow your examples. I pray that this book will be counted among my efforts to help others find truth and discover the faith, hope, and love that God offers to anyone who desires it.

Introduction

What does it mean to have faith? Most people think that to believe is to have faith. Faith and belief are most definitely related—no one can have faith without believing. But merely believing is not faith. Believing has an element of faith, but faith is not necessary to believe. For example, it takes no faith to believe that the chair I'm about to sit in will sustain me. Knowledge of the structural integrity of the chair is what allows me to confidently sit in it. Belief is based on knowledge and/or experience. Faith, however, is quite different.

Faith is acting on what we believe. To illustrate, based on experience we believe that the sun will rise tomorrow, so we make plans. We can't know for certain that the sun will rise until we actually see it rise. Making plans before the sun rises is a demonstration of our faith. Whether we're conscious of it or not, faith determines our every decision and action in life. Faith is action- based conviction. It is our personal worldview, demonstrated.

Many people claim to have faith in a particular religious belief. Yet judging by their actions, they either don't understand the tenets of the particular religion they claim or, way down, perhaps below conscious thought, they don't really believe. They may have some doubts or questions that are unresolved. They may have merely accepted a religious belief that others important to them claim to follow. No matter the reason, there are many people who only claim to have faith in a particular religious belief. In reality, based on their actions, what they claim to believe and what they actually do believe are at odds. Based on my own experience, this concerns me greatly.

For nearly the first thirty years of my life, I thought I was a Christian. When asked, I clearly stated that I was a Christian. It wasn't until my faith was put to a serious test that I realized I had only professed to be a Christian. There were many aspects of the Christian faith of which I had no knowledge. Moreover, there were other popular beliefs and convictions I also held without realizing they were in direct opposition to the tenets of the Christian faith. Somehow, I'd never taken the time to examine what I believed or why I believed it. Instead, I suppressed fears and doubts when they surfaced and continued on believing as I did. There came a day, which I share about in chapter one, when this no longer worked. I was forced to examine my beliefs in order to find peace and have any hope at all.

What about you? If your faith were put to a test—if you encountered a faith challenging crisis today—would your faith sustain you? Are you confident about what you believe and why you believe it? Have you intentionally taken the time to seriously consider your faith conviction? I don't want you to come to a crisis in your life only to find that your faith is faulty—I don't want your faith to fail you when you need it the most.

I realize that not everyone who reads this book will agree with my findings. But I do hope you will seriously consider why you believe what you believe so that you can be confident in your faith, especially when you need it the most.

This book is based on two core premises: the belief that human beings intrinsically desire truth, and the belief that our soul and spirit are eternal. As humans, we hold in common an undeniable desire to discover and live in truth. Additionally, as humans, we are both mortal and immortal—our bodies are mortal while our spirit and soul are eternal. I realize some people do not believe that the human soul and spirit are everlasting. But even that belief is an aspect of faith that deserves examination.

If you are not sure that your faith is based on a solid foundation, then by all means, you should examine your faith! Finding truth in a deceptive world is possible. A renewed faith producing real hope and certain joy is available. And it's exactly what "the Faith Doctor" (this author) prescribes for you within the contents of this book.

Part One

Defending Truth

Chapter One

A Crisis of Faith

It was dark by the time I got home. Once inside, I dropped my purse and keys to the floor and closed the door by simply leaning back against it. Hearing it latch, I stumbled over to the couch and collapsed on it. The pain was unlike any other. There were times I felt completely numb and utterly mindless. This was followed by onslaughts of sheer agony with waves of memories from different times in my life. Hot, uncontrollable tears streamed down my face, while sobs and groans came from a depth of my soul that I didn't even know existed.

It was more than the fact that David, the man I believed was the one I would marry, broke off our relationship. It was the accumulation of all my life's pain—pain I'd brought on myself and pain imposed upon me. Ever since I was a very small girl, my determined purpose in life was to grow up and get married to finally satisfy this deep inner longing to be securely loved. The violence, alcoholism, and abandonment by my father carved that determination deep within me.

This night, experiencing the greatest heartache I'd ever known, I questioned everything I'd ever believed and ever hoped in. It was as though there were three of me poring over my entire life—one who was compassionate, one who was condemning, and one who was observing it all. With each memory of a different painful life experience, there was struggle for a proper understanding. My thoughts drifted further and further back. I don't know how long I'd been contemplating my life, but I seemed to have finally arrived at a memory in time that made some sense.

My parents weren't particularly religious, though both had been brought up in homes with at least a moderate respect for religious faith. My mother's family brand of Christianity leaned toward Pentecostalism. My father's family claimed to believe in Christianity, but as expressed through the Masons and Eastern Star. However, there was no evidence of this in our family life, just the retrospective awareness. The 1960s were a time when everything "established" was challenged—religion, government, marriage, sexual morals. Ethics and values of every kind were challenged and most were exploited while people "searched to find themselves." It wasn't uncommon in that cultural environment for parents let children "find their own way," which was how my sister and I were raised.

Early in my childhood my parents let us attend church with the neighbors next door. I liked getting dressed up and going to Sunday school. The teacher there was kind and gentle, but mostly it was the sense of peace in that place that I liked. As I grew, I very occasionally attended church with an aunt or other family member. By the time I was a teenager in the 1970s, exploring different beliefs and practices was the norm. There were no rules, no shoring, and no anchor. What became known as "the Jesus Movement" occurred at the same time that Hare Krishna and Eastern mysticism were promoted by various media personalities; perhaps most influential was the rock band The Beatles. Like most, I was influenced by it all.

In my quest to satiate my intense inner longing to be securely loved, I had three long-term relationships that ended in heartache. In my mid-twenties, I finally recognized that I was my own nemesis.

Without realizing it, I was attracted to men who were very much like my father—abusive, alcoholic, and unfaithful. Apparently it's very common for children to grow up and seek that which is familiar, even if it's not in their own best interest. I decided to take time to work on my own personal issues, which paid off. It took three years, but I figured out so much. So when I met David, who had no reputation for being abusive, alcoholic or unfaithful, I felt perfectly safe to pursue the relationship.

We were inseparable for just about a year. I'd never been so happy or hopeful, and I believed I was on my way to having what I'd deeply longed for all my life. David's most unexpected announcement to break off our relationship utterly and completely broke me.

I have no idea how long I'd been lying on my couch when I very clearly remembered my time in Sunday school. I recalled the teacher explaining that Jesus could come into my heart and be my "forever friend" to help me in my life. She explained that He could save me from my sins and keep me from going to eternal hell, which she made clear was a very terrible place. At the tender age of around five years, I didn't actually understand sin, but because of my home life, I knew what a terrible place was. So I did as the teacher invited us to: I asked Jesus to come into my heart to be my forever friend.

If all that was true, I pondered, then why has my life been one heartache after another? I had said the prayer as the teacher taught us. Was Jesus my friend? Was Jesus even who the Sunday school teacher said He was? Was the Bible true? Is God real?

In the greatest pain I'd ever known, alone in my living room, I found myself praying: "God, Heavenly Father, Jesus, if You are who the Sunday school teacher told me You are, if You are truly the good, loving, and merciful God who can make sense out of my life, then I need You to, now more than ever. I admit that I have really only thought of You as my Savior to keep me from hell. I haven't wanted You to be Lord of my life. But tonight I'm willing to surrender to You completely. If You can make something good out of my life, then I need You to, because on my own I've only proven that I can't."

What happened next was something I had never experienced before and haven't in the same way since. I heard the voice of God clearly speak to me. It wasn't an audible voice. It was spirit to spirit. I've since taken time to write down what was I believe He spoke to me in order to share with others. This is what I heard from God that night: "Pamela, you only understand in part. I brought David into your life, and also took him out of your life to confirm to you that it is not an earthly relationship you deeply long for—you long for Me. You met Me once a long time ago. Don't you remember? You were very little. You learned about Me from that Sunday school your parents let you attend with the neighbors. Remember? I promised you that I would never leave or forsake you. I know you remember. You gave yourself to Me then. But through the years, My heart has been repeatedly rent because you have sought the love you need in many other ways— career, position, material possessions, relationships. Yet, I have kept My promise. Though you have never acknowledged Me in your heart of hearts—you only see Me as Savior for your eternal future—I AM the God of yesterday, today and tomorrow. Now Pamela, I will wait no longer. Today, I have removed from you that which you perceive to be what you deeply long for so that you can finally and abruptly see the truth about who and what you really need."

My tears stopped flowing. My soul was quieted. I had a profound sense of peace. And the deep inner longing within me was finally and completely satisfied. In awe, I remained motionless, gratefully reflecting on what God had just said to me, pondering it and cherishing it, confident in the truth of His words.

From this, I had to know more about God. I realized that through my exposure to God as a young girl, I merely knew *about* Him. Now, I wanted to *personally know* Him. This started my journey to find truth. I had an entire life of cultivated beliefs—many of which I had merely accepted without any consideration. I had unanswered questions, doubts, and fears that I now wanted to find answers to. I had friends from faiths other than Christianity who talked about God. What made the distinctions between different religious faiths? Are we all worshiping the same God just with different expressions? What about what I'd been taught about each person finding their own truth, since what is true for one person is not necessarily true for someone else? I had so many questions that could no longer be left unanswered.

It's taken years for me to learn what is represented in this book. Some has been gained through academic study. However, the faith that has the deepest roots is that which has been tested. I am grateful to say that today my faith is stronger than ever. I have a confident faith that has been developed through challenges that now allows me to overcome adversity as never before. As is true for everyone, first I had to establish a confident conviction about the object of my faith, which is the subject of this book—**Believing Faith**. Then I had to grow and strengthen my faith to experience victory over obstacles in this life—**Effective Faith.** This will be the focus of my second in this three-book series. The second book is entitled *Renew Your Hope! Remedy for Personal Breakthroughs.* The third book planned for this series, *Revive Your Life! Rest for Your Anxious Heart,* will be about faith motivated by love—God's love. This is what I call **Excellent Faith.**

What about you? Have you ever asked basic questions about your beliefs? Have you ever truly examined what you believe and why you believe it? It took what was a series of crises for me to finally,

6

honestly explore what I believed. Will you allow your own unanswered questions to remain? Will it require a crisis that challenges what you believe to cause you to examine your faith? I pray not. Because of my experiences, I have a deep passionate desire to help people discover and live in truth. Why wait for a crisis when I can help?

I want you to allow this book to help you examine your faith. It is not my desire to tell you what to believe; rather, it is to help you intentionally come to your own beliefs. At the same time, because of the path of discovery I've taken, I openly share with you what I believe and why. I'm confident that every right-minded human being wants to discover and live in truth. It is, therefore, vitally important that we make a consorted effort to learn about truth.

The next chapter will help you take the first step in finding truth for yourself.

Chapter Two

Faith in Crisis

I have been teaching matters of faith for many years now. I have noticed a trend that disturbs me greatly. In fact, it was my reading about Americans' responses to religious diversity that became the catalyst for the timing of writing this book.

Religious diversity is the trend I am concerned about. "What?" you may ask. "That smacks of intolerance!" But carefully consider what I read about Rabbi David Ingber. He was raised in Orthodox Judaism and departed from the faith in his twenties. On his self-described spiritual journey, he practiced various aspects of Eastern religions. Ultimately he returned to his Jewish roots, bringing with him these Eastern concepts and practices. He has since become a rabbi and founded a congregation in New York City named Romemu. His slogan is *Judaism for mind, body, and spirit.* When interviewed, Ingber explained, "I do think that there's a level of maturity involved in being so secure in your own root tradition that you can dabble, that you can borrow, and that you don't feel that it's in some way sacrificing your own identity. There is a way for those who love God to love God together, and I think that's what we're trying to do now—we're trying to say, let's go beyond the labels."[1] On the surface this sounds good; after all, *tolerance* is an essential and politically correct aspect of present-day American culture.

Tolerance, however, is only as good as the wisdom behind it. Consider the wisdom of tolerating an open flame near gasoline. There is none, unless the desired outcome is a catastrophically devastating explosion.

Exploring Religious Tolerance

Religious tolerance, in popular wisdom, is respecting people's individual rights to believe what they choose to believe. Traditionally, this has been demonstrated by people from specific religious groups respecting the rights of others to belong to any religious group they choose. This is a basic religious freedom, and a core premise upon which America was founded that must be highly valued and protected for everyone.

But according to the Pew Research Center's Forum on Religion and Public Life, Americans' embrace of religious tolerance today is unique in contrast to times past. Rather than accepting religious faiths, philosophies, and ideals as distinct groups, postmodern Americans selectively accept aspects of various beliefs and practices, incorporating them together as they choose. The attempt to reconcile or bring into union different or opposing ideals, principles, and philosophies of religions is referred to as *syncretism*. And in America, the appeal for this is on the rise. Ingber said, "I do think that there's a level of maturity involved in being so secure in your own root tradition that you can dabble, that you can borrow, and that you don't feel that it's in some way sacrificing your own identity." I couldn't disagree with him more. I wholeheartedly believe it is utterly sacrificing one's identity over to deception. (I will explain more about this later.) Yet many are attracted to syncretism.

The Pew Research Center further reported, "Large numbers of Americans engage in multiple religious practices, mixing elements of diverse traditions."[2] The create-your-own-religion mentality reveals that "culture and pop-culture and the Internet are probably more powerful teachers than Sunday school teachers," according to Scott Thumma, a sociologist at the Hartford Institute of Religion Research.[3] And according to Alan Cooperman, associate director at the Pew Forum, "It is as much now the norm as it is the exception for Americans to blend multiple religious beliefs and practices. The way we personalize our iPhones, we also personalize our religious lives."[4] Like selecting from a menu at a Chinese restaurant—two from column A, three from column B and two from column C—a growing number of Americans are choosing their faith according to their own personal preferences. This type of religious diversity is increasing in America, and, sadly, a growing number of people view this as a good thing.

This concerns me greatly for several reasons. To start with, attempting to mix aspects of different faiths is evidence of the lack of core convictions. Lack of core convictions means a person cannot rely upon their faith with confidence. Moreover, when examining the basic tenets of different faiths, it becomes apparent that their selected beliefs are completely at odds with each other—there is no way to harmonize them. Finally, believing that the faith we adopt has both temporal and eternal implications makes this an extremely serious issue.

Most people believe that our human existence is eternal—that our physical life is temporal and that our soul and spirit are eternal. Further, most hold that our belief system in this life determines the ultimate eternal dwelling place of our soul and spirit.

Yet, with no apparent consideration for conflicting beliefs, Americans are combining Christianity with Eastern mysticism, New Age, astrology, and humanist beliefs—or any combination of beliefs. For some, it's an attempt to cover all the bases in the hope that at least something will enable them to go to heaven. But for most, according to the research referenced above, it's a matter of choosing what they like and disregarding what they don't like. In reality, this produces a faith founded on personal preferences that is wrought with serious conflict.

My crisis of faith shared in the previous chapter abruptly forced me to question everything I ever believed. Everything I had ever hoped for—everything I was living for. That was the most dreadful and desperate experience I have ever known. I cried out to God through my limited knowledge of Jesus. Had God not spoken to my spirit, I really don't know if I would be here today. With the seed of hope planted in me, and a compelling sense of urgency, I set myself on a steely quest. I learned a great deal—with more still to be learned. Nonetheless, what I possess now is a confident faith that is *knowingly* based on truth. For the first nearly thirty years of my life, I thought I had solid basis for building my life and my future hopes. In reality, I had a collection of beliefs that I liked without ever actually considering them—without scrutinizing their validity. Perhaps you haven't taken the time or applied the effort to examine *why* you believe what you believe. If you were to face a crisis where you truly needed your faith, would it sustain you?

Discovering Deception

With a heart wanting others to have a confident faith, one of the first questions I ask an audience when I speak in person is, "Who in this room wants to live your life on the basis of a lie?" No one ever raises their hand to that question. I then propose that unless we intentionally and regularly examine what we believe and why we believe it, we could very easily be determining our faith and subjecting our eternal lives on the basis of lies.

How can people confidently hold to a worldview they've never actually considered? Part of the reason, in my opinion, is because our public education system has come to teach people *what* to think, rather than *how* to think. It used to be that grammar (effective sentence structure), logic (reason, judgment, and common sense), and rhetoric (the art of communicating through speaking) were required fundamental pillars of basic education. But now, unless a person is a philosophy major, logic and reason are not required subjects at all!

Today, society is largely composed of people who have been "trained" instead of educated, and the result is that we have tremendous numbers of people—even in positions of leadership—who are deceived and leading others into deception without realizing it. The very nature of deception means that the victim is unaware. If you are deceived, you won't know it. I didn't know it.

When I discovered that my religious beliefs were wrought with falsehoods, I was shocked to realize I'd been living my life and making important decisions, every day, with beliefs founded on lies. This was tremendously upsetting! How could I have been so duped? I'm reasonably intelligent. I'm aptly educated. Then I realized the only way well-meaning and reasonably intelligent people can be deceived is for there to be a sufficient amount of truth-appeal within the deception.

Highly educated people are deceived. People in positions of tremendous influence and leadership are deceived. Young, old, rich, and poor are deceived. Deception is no respecter of persons. Unless a person deliberately and consciously makes the effort to examine their beliefs, they could easily be deceived. I don't want that for you. Keep reading.

Are All Religions Equal?

Once I intentionally sought to learn the truth about God and humanity, I found myself on a journey that was accelerated with every new discovery. I learned that modern *religious pluralism* (the idea that all roads lead to heaven, in an effort to combine all religions) seeks to have all religions considered equal and to attain religious unity. This appeals to our American sense of fairness. But as I continued learning, it became glaringly apparent that it is impossible to combine different religious beliefs without requiring serious compromise from each respective belief.

America's founding fathers knew that religious unity is not possible. In response, they sought to create a government that allowed for religious diversity. This was in keeping with their view that each human being is created equal and endowed by his/her Creator with certain inalienable rights. Moreover, America's founders worked hard to escape specific religious "unity demands" of the British government. Religious freedom that allows individuals to worship as they choose is an inalienable right (a right based on natural law that cannot be taken away, denied, or transferred). This right is protected in America's Bill of Rights and codified in the Constitution of the United States of America.

America's founding fathers sought unity through unique and distinctive moral and governmental ideas, which inspired the fabric of American government—ideas such as inalienable rights, individualism, limited government, full republicanism, separation of powers, checks and balances, and an educated and virtuous citizenry. Those ideas produced a national unity that encompassed America's great diversity of race, ethnicity, and religion.[5] In the founding of America, Judeo-Christian values were the bedrock for governmental and national ideals with the right for people to maintain other religious faith completely protected.

Erwin W. Lutzer, in his book *Christ Among Other gods: A Defense of Christ in an Age of Tolerance,* offers an explanation of how the movement for America to become pluralistic has grown. In 1993, he attended the Parliament of the World's Religions that met in Chicago. Lutzer writes, "With lofty ideals and utopian plans to unify the religions of the world for the common good, this parliament met to break down the barriers that exist in the accelerated march toward religious unity. Six thousand delegates came to learn from one another, explore areas of agreement, and grasp a better understanding of one another's religious heritages." The premise in the minds of virtually all in attendance was that "it doesn't matter what god you pray to, because every deity is ultimately the same deity shrouded in a different name."[6]

The efforts of this parliament echoed a religious viewpoint that has existed for thousands of years under different names such as *ecumenism, traditionalism,* or *perennialism.* The parliament described what was then representative of a minority of people, but that today seems to be increasing by leaps and bounds. This perspective was confirmed with the 1993–1994 Barna research report, which indicated that nearly two out of three adults contend that the choice of one religious faith over another is irrelevant, because all religions teach the same basic lessons about life.[7]

J. P. Moreland, distinguished professor of philosophy at Talbot School of Theology, wrote about an unnamed student's response to the discussion of the specific claims of Jesus. The student's response was, "I think Jesus is great for you, but I know Buddhists and Muslims, and they're just as sincere as you are. And they think their views are true just like you do. There's no way a person can know his religion is the 'right' one, so the best thing to do is to just believe everyone's religion is true for them and not judge anyone."[8] Aware of it or not, this student echoed the view of religious pluralism.

Especially important to the secular point of view is the acceptance of all religions as equal. It's not enough to tolerate the existence of different religions—we must accept them all as equally valid. And if one can't quite accept that all religions are equally valid, then at the least, in today's cultural climate, one must adhere to *inclusivism* (open to other religions). Inclusivism is a movement that began with the eighteenth-century Enlightenment. This Enlightenment movement declares that ignorance and narrow-mindedness would limit "God's" revelation to only one particular faith group. Inclusivism has brought Americans to *selectivism*, which, according to Lutzer, teaches that we "must not follow any one religion, but compile our own personal list of cherished beliefs."[9]

Increasingly, today's generation wants to take religion out of the realm of rational discourse and relegate it to the area of personal preferences and opinions. If there are thirty-one different flavors of ice cream, why not have variety in religions? The gods of the New Age movement are always tolerant of sexual preferences, feminism, and hedonistic pleasures at almost any cost. Why shouldn't people choose a religion that is compatible with their private values? Americans have become caught up in the belief that in order to have meaningful faith, it must agree with their deeply held personal preferences.

The bitter pill of deception has been sugar-coated with what appeals to us carnally—that is, what appeals to us physically and especially sexually. We have become a society that makes decisions on the basis of what we subjectively or emotionally feel rather than what we have objectively reasoned.

In today's politically correct climate, it is assumed that no one is in any position to judge another. But in doing this, we permit ourselves, and those we love, to be deceived. In reality, without objective principles to guide our chosen beliefs, any choice is either purely arbitrary or totally based on emotion or upbringing.

Examining the Evidence

Francis Collins, one of the world's leading geneticists and well known for heading the Human Genome Project, became a medical doctor after completing his doctorate in chemistry at Yale. In the early years of his medical practice, when treating patients facing death who confidently declared their faith, he realized he had never really examined the evidence for his atheistic belief. This bothered him, because as a scientist he was trained to draw conclusions based on facts and examine the evidence. In his effort to confirm that God does not exist, he came across the writings of C. S. Lewis, who himself was once an atheist.

Collins writes about reading Lewis's book, *Mere Christianity:*

> It took me three or four months to get all the way through that book, because it was very unsettling to see that the foundations of my atheism were falling apart page by page and leaving me in a position of having to accept the idea of God's existence: something that I was not prepared for.

> It was Lewis's argument about the moral law, this knowledge of right and wrong that distinguishes us from all other species, that I found most convincing and do to this day. It is a moral law that we break quite regularly, but we know it's there. It often makes very little sense in naturalistic terms because it sometimes calls us to do acts of radical self-sacrifice (like risking

your own life to save another's), that are clearly not good for the passing on of our DNA, which is all that evolution by natural selection would care about. That part of the argument led me to acknowledge that if God exists, then God cares about people. Why else would this moral law be something that people, including me, experience?[10]

In his book *The Language of God: A Scientist Presents Evidence for Belief,* Collins shared how he came to realize that scientific evidence points to God as Creator, a good, loving, and holy God, who calls us all to be good, loving, and holy (morally, physically, and spiritually).

When I ask my audiences, "Who in this room wants to live your life on the basis of a lie?" I discover some very important matters. Since no one ever raises their hand, the reality of our commonly preferring truth becomes evident. This means that we, as human beings, have an intuitive moral compass. We intuitively want to live our life on the basis of what is true and good, over living it on the basis of what is false and bad.

Morality and truth are two topics that have been bandied about. Yet unless we discover actual truth, morality is up for grabs. This explains the condition of America today.

Clearly, both good and evil coexist in this world. Religions and philosophies attempt to identify the origin of good and evil and human existence, and then propose methods to overcome evil in order to live what is good—physically, emotionally, mentally, and spiritually.

Regardless of what you believe, whether you follow a particular religious group or have joined the increasing number of Americans who develop their faith based on personal preferences, it is vitally important to examine why you believe as you do, not only to have every opportunity to live life today in what is "good," but so you can be confident of where your life is taking you in the hereafter.

Your personal beliefs, your faith, are an integrated part of you—they are the very essence of who you are. Every day you consciously and subconsciously base decisions on your personal beliefs. Your parents and other significant people in your life have influenced what you believe today, so to examine what you believe can feel like an affront to them. This can be quite unsettling. If you discover that what you believe is faulty, then you have to admit that you've been wrong—and that's not easy! It takes real courage, and it can be painful to examine what you believe. But not to do so is to choose to be willfully ignorant.

If you choose not to examine what you believe and why you believe it, then you are knowingly subjecting yourself to the prospect of deception. Although examining your personal faith is difficult, I suspect that you know in your heart of heart's it's the wise thing to do.

Faith in America is definitely in a crisis. Never has there been a time of greater moral decline, social unrest, economic uncertainty, distrust of leadership, and disgust with media, or a time where confident faith has been needed more.

You can recover from deceptive thinking simply by intentionally and regularly examining what you believe and why you believe it. Only then can you be sure you are basing your life—*your eternal life*—on what is good.

Let's explore this more together. By our journey's end, I'm confident you'll be equipped with a faith that won't fail you when you need it the most.

Chapter Three

Faith and Truth

I recently sat across a massive mahogany conference table in a room with floor-to-ceiling bookshelves crammed with all sorts of beautifully bound books. Listening to a man with an impressive list of accomplishments, I was taken aback when he said, "I don't have time to deal with stupid." He paused, then continued, "In this age of easily accessible information, there's no reason for a person to be stupid. I can't waste my time dealing with stupid."

By "stupid," he in no way meant a person who was learning impaired. He meant people who choose to remain improperly informed. That was clear from his next statement: "It's one thing for a person to do something stupid, be willing to learn from it, and make a course correction. It's quite another for a person to slothfully remain stupid!"

He echoed my heart, especially concerning the matter of faith. And in my experience many people are, in fact, improperly informed when it comes to understanding what faith is.

The Definition of Faith Is What?

To prove my point, at your computer using a simple Google search, enter the phrase "define the word faith." You'll be taken to a list of online dictionaries. When I tried this, the first site listed on the search was a free dictionary promoted as the "world's most comprehensive" dictionary. They make this claim based on their use of multiple sources for their published data with "a large part of the information being checked and edited by their staff" http://www.thefreedictionary.com/ faith. Following are the first two definitions listed for the word *faith*:

> Confident belief in the truth, value, or trustworthiness of a person, idea, or thing.

> Belief that does not rest on logical proof or material evidence.

These are two very different definitions of a single word. For both definitions to be correct, a person would have to be confident of a truth, value, or trustworthiness of a person, idea, or thing without any logical proof or material evidence. No one in their right mind does that! We can only have confident belief in the truth, value, or trustworthiness of a person or a matter once it's been determined trustworthy.

We oftentimes take action with the *hope* that a person or matter is trustworthy, but that's not faith. It's hope. Any faith conviction requires sufficient substantiation to allow a person to confidently act on their faith.

I checked the definition of faith from the next dictionary listed. The first two definitions listed on http://dictionary.reference.com/ browse/faith are:

> Confidence or trust in a person or thing: faith in another's ability.

> Belief that is not based on proof: He had faith that the hypothesis would be substantiated by fact.

Again, the first definition is accurate *if* the confidence or trust was sufficiently determined or proven in advance. But definition two from this second dictionary is more accurately the definition of hope: *He had hope that the hypothesis would be substantiated by fact.*

A definition of sound faith that I've come up with is this: A belief that has a sufficient amount of objective verifiable evidence to allow a person to subjectively believe that which is not yet proven. There is a measure of the "unknown" to faith, but it is overshadowed by what is confidently known. Confident belief for what is not yet proven, or that which is not yet experienced, can only exist once a person has sufficient objective, verifiable evidence and/or experience allowing him or her to believe what doesn't yet subsist. What convinces a person to place or establish faith in anyone or anything is a sufficient amount of objective, verifiable information and/or experience. The term *sufficient* is key—what is sufficient for one may not be for someone else. Regardless, faith combined with sufficient objective, verifiable evidence results in an unwavering conviction—a confident faith.

Feeling Versus Thinking

The pursuit of sound faith and convincing truth today is not as easily completed as in times past. Under the postmodern banner of tolerance, respect for what a person feels is of great importance. We have even changed our language. We use the phrase "I feel" when in context the phrase should be "I think." There is intentionality in saying, "I feel," because no one can challenge what another person feels. Feelings are subjective, whereas thoughts are determined by objective information. Tell me what you feel and I have to accept it. Tell me what you think and I can challenge you. What greatly concerns me is the growing number of people who claim to "feel" or, more accurately, believe things that are in opposition to reality.

Thinking clearly and properly, using reason and logic to interpret objective evidence, is the beginning of forming one's faith—*if the intention is to have sound faith.* If a person would rather have a feel-good faith with no concern for the validity of it, then leading with feelings or personal preferences is the way to go.

If we seek to develop our faith with a proper distinction between thinking and feeling, we have a better chance of establishing a sound faith. Thinking *should be* based on objective facts. Feelings *are* based on subjective principles and values. Our thinking can be skewed by our feelings. And our feelings can be subjected to our thoughts. In fact, the successful subjection of our feelings to our thoughts is what allows a person to rate better in what has become known as the Emotional Management Scale.[1]

Dr. Daniel Goleman, a psychologist, best-selling author, and lecturer, is largely accredited with raising current awareness about *emotional intelligence.* Most people are more familiar with the intelligence quotient (IQ), which is a measure of one's cognitive abilities, such as the ability to learn or understand new situations, how to reason through a given problem/scenario, and the ability to apply knowledge to one's current situations. It involves primarily the neocortex, or top portion of the brain. The emotional quotient is a measure of one's emotional intelligence, as defined by the ability to use both emotional and cognitive thought. Emotional intelligence skills include but are not limited to empathy, intuition, creativity, flexibility, resilience, stress management, leadership, integrity, authenticity, intrapersonal skills, and interpersonal skills. It involves the lower and central sections of the brain called the limbic system.[2]

While I don't personally accept all the significance many ascribe to the emotional quotient, I do recognize the importance of our decisions being made using both our cognitive thought process and our emotional understandings.

If you have not drawn on both intentional cognitive thinking and mature emotional discretion, you could easily have a faith that is faulty. Unless you courageously examine what you believe and why you believe it, you won't know if your faith is accurate until it is tested. Waiting until then could prove very costly. Just like having automobile insurance in place before you have an accident, faith needs to be properly intact before there's a need to draw on it.

We previously concluded that no one would intentionally choose to live his/her life on the basis of lies. We commonly agree that to do so would be bad. All of us want to live our life on the basis of truth, which we commonly agree is good. But choosing good over bad, or right instead of wrong, depends upon our concept of truth. One's understanding of truth has a direct impact on morality and culture. *Truth* is another word that suffers ambiguous definition.

Is Truth Relative?

Can truth be relative? Many people claim that truth is relative. *Relativism* is the view that there are no fixed reference points by which morality and religion can be judged. Relativists purport that one's point of view can *only* be relative and subjective because it is influenced by some particular frame of reference such as language or culture. "Beauty is in the eye of the beholder" is one example in support of subjective perception.

Relativists claim that all points of view are equally valid. What one person believes to be truth is his/her personal truth and not necessarily what is accepted as truth for someone else. Again, in this age of tolerance, on the surface this sounds so noble. And for this reason, relativism has gained in popularity. But popularity in and of itself doesn't determine accuracy. Let's next examine the claim that all truth is relative.

Relativists say, "What you believe to be true is your truth and what I believe to be truth is my truth," *even if the two beliefs are at complete odds.*

Relativists also make this claim: "There is no such thing as absolute truth," *yet that statement is itself an absolute statement about truth.*

Relativists claim to esteem all points of view as equally valid, *except absolutism.*

The relativist believes that subjective truth is true for everyone, but this is the one thing they cannot believe. If a relativist thinks it is true for everyone, then he believes it is an absolute truth. Therefore, he is no longer a relativist.

According to relativism, if Billy Graham believes God exists and an atheist believes God does not exist, both would be right. With subjective truth, no one could ever be wrong since there is no single standard for right and wrong. As long as something is true to the holder of a particular truth, it is true for them, even if it is wrong for someone else.

The growing popularity of tolerating contradictory points of view is precisely what is contributing to the cultural moral chaos we're suffering today. The morality of mankind (choosing right from wrong) is based on our concept of truth.

When we examine the Holocaust and question the morality of this event, we are confronted with the basis for truth used by Hitler's Nazi Germany. After World War II, this was one of the questions seriously contemplated at the Nuremberg trials. The basis for truth used by Nazi Germany was the Darwinian principle of the survival of the fittest. The leaders of Germany saw their nation as a superior group—"Stronger People"—and the rest of the world as an inferior people—"Weaker People." Friedrich Nietzsche, a German philosopher whose influence is substantial to this day, taught that man is the source for good and evil.

Nietzsche, also well known for his radical questioning of the value and objectivity of truth, had tremendous influence on Hitler. The questions faced by the Nuremburg trials are the same questions we face today: "What truth is the basis of our moral law?" and "Is truth subjective or objective?" If truth is relative, then morality can be relative.[3] Subjective truth is not only irrational, it's also exceedingly dangerous.

Relativism allows the individual to be his/her own supreme authority—each person decides for himself/herself what is right and what is wrong. This is the same thought behind people forming their "faith" on the basis of personal preferences. With subjective feelings as the basis for conviction, any claim a relativist makes cannot be successfully refuted by anyone else. Only the person knows his/her own feelings. Feelings cannot be challenged or debated the same way objective thought can.

As an experiment, take notice of how often people use the phrase "I feel" instead of "I think." For a full day or during a group conversation, make a point of noting when a person says, "I feel." Using this statement has become the preferred terminology. Why? Because "I feel" declarations are statements of personal entitlement that can't be challenged. A person's feelings are to be highly respected in a culture that promotes tolerance. So "I feel" statements are preferred because they allow the individual to be his/her own authority.

The idea of being one's own authority is another deception that that is sugar-coated. The natural pride of the individual self does not like being told what to do. Not one of us naturally likes the idea of submitting to authority. When we choose to do so, we give rational consent, believing that the resulting order is the better outcome—it is good.

Yet, under the banner of relativism, without any subjective standard, everyone is free to affirm even a demonic god, and no one else has any authority to say he or she is wrong. In my considered opinion, relativism is the modern-day catalyst for deceptive thinking leading to the increase of all that is bad.

Regardless of what a relativist claims to be true, real-world laws exist that reveal that truth is objective and it exists beyond us. For example, a person can claim he can fly all they want, but once he jumps off a cliff, the natural law of gravity proves the truth. These natural laws are important to consider in our quest for truth. Now don't allow yourself to get lost in what follows. Read it at your own pace, ponder what's written, then move on to understand the next law as you're ready. What follows are known as the Laws of Rational Thought.

Is the Truth Absolute?

Once I started on this journey to learn all I could about truth, there was no stopping me. I listened to religious teaching and talk radio all day long every day. I went to seminars. I enrolled at Biola University's certification course in apologetics. *Apologetics* is an academic word that simply means "defending the faith." If you want a more in-depth definition, it is a systematic argument or discourse in the defense of faith—any faith or doctrine. In the search for truth, we are subject to specific laws. In the same way that we are subject to various laws of physics, we are subject to other natural laws. These are known as the Laws of Rational Thought:

The Law of Non-Contradiction (A is not non-A): Opposite truth claims cannot both be true. For example, if an atheist believes God does not exist and a theist believes God does exist, it is impossible for both to be right.

The Law of Excluded Middle (either A or non-A): This asserts that it is either A or non-A, but not both. God cannot exist and not exist. In other words, there is no middle ground; opposites cannot be the same.

The Law of Identity (A is A): This law simply states that something is what we say it is: A is A. When someone says, "I loved the book," it is understood to mean a "book" (and not a duck or an automobile). Without the law of identity, there would be chaos and language would be incoherent.[4]

There is an absolute standard regarding any truth, though not everyone is willing to accept it. To confirm that a matter is truth, three essential characteristics must be in place at the same time:

1. The truth is based in reality.
2. Only one thing can be true and all opposing matters are false.
3. The truth is universal.

As a mother of two, I had more than one occasion where my children sought to create a truth they preferred, generally in attempt to avoid a consequence they knew was "bad." You can imagine the scenario that would cause me to say, "Sorry sweetie, but the chocolate crumbs on your hands and face provide evidence that you did eat the last of the cookies."

What is the application of discovering truth?

1. All the cookies are gone—the truth is based in reality.
2. The cookies can't both be in the jar and gone at the same time—one matter is true, all opposing matters are false.
3. Based on the evidence of a precious child's face covered with cookie crumbs, any mother in the world would come to the same conclusion—the truth is universal.

In this postmodern American culture, discovering the truth may be more difficult than ever, but it is still not impossible, nor does it require genius. We must rationally examine all truth claims. Every religion and philosophy has the responsibility of giving evidence for its truth claims, and such evidence should be available for believers and unbelievers—the burden of proof is on the claimant.[5]

People who choose to maintain beliefs based on their personal preferences have a general sense they are operating with ideals contrary to most others. The only way they can alleviate this is to seek to change the beliefs of others. As in the example of my children and the missing cookies, they work very hard to substantiate their claims, seeking to convince others that their beliefs are valid and deserving of respect and should therefore bring no negative consequences.

One of the ways people seek to have their truth claims acknowledged by others is to attempt to alter reality in the minds of those who oppose their beliefs. *Revisionism* is one such tactic. Public school textbooks, for example, have been revised as a means to indoctrinate the most impressionable in society: our children.

Consider how evolution is taught in public schools today as fact, not theory, while the Creation account for the origin of humanity is taught as a fairy tale. Clearly this is not teaching with respect to individual intelligence or using sound logic and reason. What should be presented are the objective facts and evidence so that the student can decide. Instead, our schools provide deductive instruction that tells students what to think rather than offer inductive instruction that encourages people how to think.

In this postmodern culture that has elevated tolerance without wisdom, claims that truth is relative are made with few people prepared to challenge or debate the claim. Until we can agree that truth is objective and verifiable, there can be no debate with relativists. Another way I like to say it: "You just can't reason with crazy."

Consider the following false objections that relativists make concerning absolute truth and the reasonable corresponding responses.

If truth is absolute, then no new truth would be possible. This mistakes the *process of discovery* with truth. People once thought the earth was flat when in reality it was a sphere. Truth is revealed or understood over a period of time. It is not altered with new information.

Absolute truth is too narrow. Any truth claim is narrow because truth by its nature means that anything that opposes it is false.

Absolute truth is dogmatic. Yes, it is, because the claim of truth excludes non-truth, which makes it reasonable to be dogmatic.

No one can know something is true. We can know if something is true based on the process of discovery. If we don't understand the truth about a matter, it doesn't alter the truth. Truth exists beyond our selves.

In conclusion, *absolute truth* stands on its own. Absolute truth is absolutely true no matter what evidence has been or is yet to be discovered. Truth corresponds to facts. Truth does not change just because we learn something new about it.[6] Truth is not subject to our feelings or opinions rather, the converse is correct.

Man has the ability to think logically and apply reason using our intellect, and at the same time has an amazing gift of imagination. The danger is when one's imagination clouds or impairs a person's ability to remain grounded in empirical truth—that is, practical, verifiable evidence from experience and not theory.

To have true, loving compassion is to want others to know the truth and live in what is good, now and forever. In the spirit of my friend at the conference table, I hope this book convinces you to proactively seek to be and remain properly informed because, as I firmly believe, your temporal and eternal life is at risk.

Chapter Four

Faith in God(s)

I grew up in the sixties and seventies and was most certainly influenced by the ideologies of the time. In the wake of the Vietnam War, "peace" was the mantra while the youth made effort to break from establishment. Perhaps The Beatles, more than any other pop culture group, gave momentum to the sentiments of the period with their song "Imagine." The lyrics invite people to imagine a world with no countries, with nothing to kill or die for, and that is void of all religion. This, the song asserts, would create peace, allowing the people of the world to live as one.

Getting rid of traditional divisive religions and destructive governmental ideals and finding a universally accepted mindset so that "the world will be as one" is a very compelling idea! I'd venture that any reasonable person is attracted to this prospect. One long-held ideal to this end that some believe is capable of accomplishing this is known as *religious pluralism.*

Understanding Religious Pluralism

Attempts to create religious pluralism have been under way in America for many decades. Religious pluralism is a movement that believes all roads lead to heaven/the same God, that all religions are equal, and that it seeks to attain religious unity. Religious pluralism attempts to operate under the principles of acceptance and diversity. It is promoted as a system "for the common good of all." But for pluralism to function with any success, all groups must come to a consensus concerning values held in common. The very premise of religious pluralism is the claim that one religion is not the sole exclusive source of values, truths, and supreme deity, with the underlying belief that some truth must exist in all other religious belief systems.

However, the claim that some truth must exist in all religious belief systems requires a careful examination of the differing beliefs to confirm if that statement is accurate. Moreover, there is the problem of consensus of values held in common, because when the respective religious beliefs are analyzed there is little that the distinct religions have in common. Regardless, the effort by some to attain religious pluralism is tenacious.

Although designs for religious pluralism have been attempted throughout the ages, in the nineteenth century scholars again made a determined effort to discover a common essence in all religions. Religious pluralism is gaining tremendous momentum in America. A quick search on the Internet revealed the following article, which contained a definition of religious pluralism, as published on the Pluralism Project website of Harvard University and attributed to Diana L. Eck:

> The plurality of religious traditions and cultures has come to characterize every part of the world today. But what is pluralism? Here are four points to begin our thinking:
>
> First, pluralism is not diversity alone, but the energetic engagement with diversity. Diversity can and has meant the Creation of religious ghettoes with little traffic between or among them. Today, religious diversity is a given, but pluralism is not a given; it is an achievement.

Mere diversity without real encounter and relationship will yield increasing tensions in our societies.

Second, pluralism is not just tolerance, but the active seeking of understanding across lines of difference. Tolerance is a necessary public virtue, but it does not require Christians and Muslims, Hindus, Jews, and ardent secularists to know anything about one another. Tolerance is too thin a foundation for a world of religious difference and proximity. It does nothing to remove our ignorance of one another, and leaves in place the stereotype, the half-truth, the fears that underlie old patterns of division and violence. In the world in which we live today, our ignorance of one another will be increasingly costly.

Third, pluralism is not relativism, but the encounter of commitments. The new paradigm of pluralism does not require us to leave our identities and our commitments behind, for pluralism is the encounter of commitments. It means holding our deepest differences, even our religious differences, not in isolation, but in relationship to one another.

Fourth, pluralism is based on dialogue. The language of pluralism is that of dialogue and encounter, give and take, criticism and self-criticism. Dialogue means both speaking and listening, and that process reveals both common understandings and real differences. Dialogue does not mean everyone at the "table" will agree with one another. Pluralism involves the commitment to being at the table—with one's commitments.[1]

The tenets of religious pluralism noted above describe the premises of the effort quite well. However, included in these premises are tremendous obstacles making the effort utterly impossible. Many of the same reasons relativism cannot be defended as reviewed in the previous chapter include the *laws of rational thought* and the three essentials required to define truth.

Regarding the Parliament of World Religions of 1994, Erwin W. Lutzer, who attended, states:

> Mind you, at the parliament, no one suggested that Christians should stop being Christians or that Hindus should stop being Hindus; nor should Buddhists stop being Buddhists. The religions of the world have a rich diversity that should be prized. Each should be admired as one beautiful petal; together they form a magnificent flower called religions, a flower that no one religion could create by itself.
>
> This flower is growing more quickly before our eyes than we realize. The soil has been prepared, the seeds have been planted, and the plant is beginning to bloom. Only mindless fanatics would spoil its beauty and energy. This flower, we are told, will bless the world.[2]

Those who esteem religious pluralism in order to find a harmony among the world religions believe:

- The doctrines of the different faiths should not be held as supreme truths; each contributes a part to the whole truth, which is supreme. It is best to speak in terms of religious traditions instead of religious truths.
- No religion should be thought of as superior to another.
- People are encouraged to retain their own particular religion but must also move beyond it to deeper levels of experience, moving us all away from religion toward spirituality.
- Seeking to win others to your own beliefs is considered bigotry.

In religious pluralism, people are encouraged to pray to their "god of choice." After all, the various religions are but different expressions of the same ultimate God (or gods). Proponents believe that religious pluralism is our only hope for world peace.

Exploring Religious Distinctions

When comparing the various tenets of the different religious faiths, it is impossible to find unity—let alone harmony—between them. Each is vastly different in their explanations of the most basic questions: Is there a God or gods? If so, how can we know? What is his/her/their disposition concerning mankind? Where did mankind come from? Is there any purpose in life? How do we solve the problem of evil?

Some religions say that God exists. Others say He doesn't exist. Some say God has a Son named Jesus. Others say God can't have a son. Some say God is personal and you can have a relationship with Him. Others say God is not personal, nor can mankind directly relate with Him.[3]

Religions differ on many other aspects as well. They differ on their concepts of heaven and hell, the existence of the spirit/soul, the existence of evil, the origin of creation and humanity, and many other core issues.[4]

Based just on what's been written above, if all religions are equally valid and true, and all lead to the same destiny, then there must be many different gods and heavens, or maybe (meaning no disrespect simply trying to make sense of the differing claims) there is one God and He is schizophrenic!

In reality, the only thing the various religions have in common is the fact that they have *almost* nothing in common. However, there is some commonality in the sense of *the reason religions exist,* which will be explored in chapter ten.

Religion is another word that is defined and used in multiple ways. I use the term to mean two things: (1) the specific outward expression/practice of one's personal faith/religious belief system, and (2) the name that describes the particular faith/belief system. By this definition, secular/nonreligious, agnostic and atheists are recognized.

The top six major world religions represent an estimated total of 3.5 to 4 billion people. Ranked by number of adherents, the top five are as follows[5]:

Christianity	2 billion
Islam	1.3 billion
Secular/nonreligious, agnostic and atheists	1.1 billion
Hinduism	900 million
Buddhism	560 million
Judaism	14 million

As of the time of writing of this book, the total number of the world population is an estimated nearly 7 billion.[6]

According to the statistics above, Christianity is the most popular of all world religions. But popularity in and of itself doesn't determine accuracy. That can only be accomplished under the microscope of scrutiny.

When examining religious faiths, it is difficult to capture the beliefs of every single member of just *one particular faith* due to doctrinal differences. Within Christianity, for example, there are countless denominations. Within Judaism, there are various groups. and likewise with Islam, Hinduism, and Buddhism. Within each major religion, there are many group distinctions or sects. However, there usually are overarching tenets that most people of the faith adhere to in some fashion. The following introduction to the distinctions various religious faiths make about "God" are by no means exhaustive, but provide a basis of comparing the different religious beliefs. In subsequent chapters, the respective religious beliefs will be more particularly and individually explored.

Judaism, Hinduism, Islam, and Christianity are theistic religions. Buddhism, secular, and New Age are atheistic religions. All differ in their teachings on God, man, evil, salvation, Jesus, heaven, and hell.

Basic Contrast of Major World Religions

In *Christianity*, as revealed in the Bible, (both Old and New Testaments), God is the only self-existent, eternal, single entity, yet a triune Being (Creator, Son, and Spirit). It is He who created, sustains, and preserves the universe, who is all-powerful, all-knowing, all-merciful, everywhere present, and loving. He ordains and judges all that occurs in the universe. He is knowable by anyone who desires to know Him through faith in Jesus (the second person of the triune God-head who offers mankind redemption/delivery from evil), and is therefore personal.

According to the *Qur'an* (also spelled *Koran*) and tradition, *Islam* believes in one God (Allah), with a heavy emphasis on Him as strictly singular, who is incomparable, eternal, all-powerful, all-knowing, all-merciful, everywhere present, self-existent, and Creator of all that exists, and who guides humanity to the right way—"the holy ways." His moral and spiritual distinctions from humanity make it necessary that He be largely removed from the events of this world. He is considered personal in that He responds whenever a person in need or distress calls Him, but He cannot be personally known. Islam teaches that Allah is the same God worshipped by members of other Abrahamic religions such as Christianity and Judaism, though Christians and Jews disagree.[7]

As a group, secular/nonreligious is referred to as *humanist*. Humanists believe either that God is "in" everyone and everything, which is what *New Age* promotes, or that God exists but is unknowable. Belief that God exists but man cannot relate to Him is the position of *agnostics*. Belief that God does not exist is the position of *atheists*. While humanism is not recognized as a religious faith, it is a belief system that many people adhere to. Much of what they believe can be found in the "Humanist Manifesto," which contains various writings by like-minded individuals.[8] Similarly, there are many written essays or documents atheists and agnostics refer to and hold in common. New Age has gained in popularity and points to books such as *A Course in Miracles* by Helen Schucman, which is fast becoming the New Age bible.

Based on the authoritative documents for *Hinduism* (the *Vedas*, *Brahmans*, and *Upanishads*), Hindus believe in many gods. It has been said of Hinduism that there are as many as three hundred thousand gods—so many that it's often called the religion of a million gods. Most devotees revere or worship a few favorites and seek to respect them all. For Hindus, these gods merely represent an impersonal force: Braham, the One, the Soul of the Cosmos, in whom believers are to lose their identity to attain this ultimate Oneness. Logic for Hindus exists on a lower plane. As followers approach the Ultimate, all distinctions vanish and everything converges into One.

Buddhism is a religion whose founder, Siddhartha Gautama, born around 500 bc, refused to speculate upon the existence of deities. The result in many Buddhist countries today is that no word exists for a supreme, divine being. Siddhartha rejected his native Hindu religion and his life of luxury to discover the solution to the suffering in this world. "Enlightenment" is the goal of practicing Buddhists. The writings based on the founder's wisdom, known as the *Tripitaka* and *Mahayana Sutras*, make up an enormous and complicated variety of texts—not one of which is considered authentic and authoritative in all schools of Buddhism. Tenets of the Buddhist faith include belief in reincarnation, the Four Noble Truths, which is the heart of

Siddhartha's teachings, and the Eightfold Path, believed to be the essential journey to end suffering.

According to the core sacred writings of *Judaism,* collectively known as the *Tanakh,* there is only one, indivisible, non-physical God who is the Creator of all that has or will ever exist. He is perfect, and is often beyond human ability to comprehend. God nevertheless interacts with mankind and the world and is present in everyday lives. God gave the Jewish people the Torah ("instructions for living"). How individual Jews choose to understand this manifestation of the divine varies. Some connect with God through prayer, others see the divine in the majesty of the natural world, others may not think about God on a daily basis. Each individual's relationship with God is unique and personal. Jews look forward to God sending the promised Deliverer to relieve His people from the sufferings of this world.[9]

Most religious faiths believe that humans are eternal beings. All but Christianity promote a methodology to earn one's way to the ultimate destination of blessedness, Nirvana, heaven, or elevated eternal dwelling state.

Within each of the major religious faiths, there are various multiple doctrines, denominations, branches, or sects. These generally hold to the most basic tenets of the particular faith, but include or exclude other beliefs and practices.

Compromise Required in Quest to Harmonize

Essentially, what religious pluralism seeks—unity among all religions—is not plausible. For this to be achieved, each religion would have to surrender its claim to truth and speak only of having a different perspective of truth in contrast to other religions. In religious pluralism no single religion is permitted to have an exclusive claim to truth—instead all religions provide an aspect of truth.

Unlike *legal tolerance* in America (which is the right for everyone to believe in whatever faith they choose), and unlike *social tolerance* (which is a commitment respecting all men even if we vigorously disagree with their religion and ideals), *uncritical tolerance* of religious pluralism avoids vigorous debate. This new tolerance insists that we have no right to disagree with a liberal social agenda—we should not defend our personal views of morality, religion, and respect for human life. While this tolerance respects absurd ideas, it will castigate anyone who believes in absolutes or who claims to have found some truth. This tolerance includes every point of view except those points of view that do not include every point of view.[10]

This new, uncritical tolerance icon of religious pluralism can be used to promote perpetual skepticism, to discount commitment to any religious faith, and to promote acceptance of the most bizarre ideas. Sadly, many Americans have mindlessly embraced these ideas which have given rapid rise to the New Age worldview. More about this perspective is presented in chapter eight.

The next six chapters provide information about the origin and traditions of the top six religions or belief systems. I have intentionally refrained from offering any personal commentary—though you will find a caution from a former New Ager in chapter eight. I seek to provide you a brief overview of each as true to the particular religious faiths. In chapter eleven, I provide personal testimonies from individuals who practiced each of the religious beliefs considered in this book. It seemed most honest for any commentary about these beliefs to come from those who had personal experience. As I wrote early in this book, it is not my desire to tell you what to think. I seek to present information to help you decide for yourself. We start our study with an overview of the faith with the least in numbers: Judaism.

Part Two

Discovering Truth

Chapter Five

Faith Findings—Judaism

Although the name of God for the Jewish people is Yahweh, out of reverence, Jews will not address or refer to Him by name, neither will they write the full name without omitting the vowels. Accordingly, when written it appears as YHWH or G-d. Therefore, from this point forward in our discussion of Judaism, I will use their form of writing when referring to G-d, except when citing a quote. If you've never gathered an overview of the Jewish faith, you should find this chapter helpful.

Origin of Judaism

Modern-day Judaism is a religious tradition with origins dating back over four thousand or more years, depending upon dates given to specific events, considered later. It is rooted in the territory near the eastern region of Canaan. Canaan is the ancient name for the area between the Jordan River and the Mediterranean, which is now Israel and Palestinian territories. At the beginning of this faith, there was no name given to the followers, collectively. Over time, they became known as the people of Israel (the second name given to Jacob, who was one of the forefathers of the faith). Later, they became known as Hebrews. Classical or rabbinic Judaism did not emerge until the first century AD.

Judaism traces its heritage to the covenant, or promise, G-d made with Abraham and his lineage—that G-d would make them a sacred people and give them a holy land. The primary figures of the Israelite culture include the *patriarchs* Abraham, Isaac, Jacob (later named Israel), and the *prophet* Moses. According to the faith, it was Moses who received G-d's law at Mt. Sinai. Judaism is a tradition grounded in the religious, ethical, and social laws as they are articulated in the Torah—the first five books of the Hebrew Scriptures.[1] The entirety of the Hebrew scriptures contains the exact same books as the Christian Old Testament.

While some claim that the Hebrew faith as a specific religion began with Moses, most Jews trace Judaism's establishment as a distinct religion back to a man with the birth name of Abram. According to Jewish tradition Abram was born in the city of Ur in Babylonia in the year 1948 from creation as the Jewish calendar records, which is 1813 BC on the Gregorian calendar.[2] The Jewish calendar is believed to mark every year in succession since the Creation of all that exists (according to their calculations). However, others outside the Jewish faith, including Dr. Ralph F. Wilson, express that there are problems in determining Abram's date of birth. As Wilson's article explains, Abram's birth could be as early as 1952 BC or as late as 2166 BC.[3] Nonetheless, most Jewish sources arrive at a date near 1800–1013 BC.

The word *Jew* can be used to mean an ethnic or cultural identity or it can have a spiritual connotation. John Dickson, author of *A Spectator's Guide to World Religions,* wrote, "Between the ancient Land of Israel and the founding of the modern State of Israel, the term 'Israel' means far more than a piece of land in the Middle East. Israel was a collective reference to members of God's chosen people, the Jews, wherever they happened to live."[4]

Early Jewish Traditions

Abram was the son of Terach—an idol merchant, according to legend. The Torah itself does not verify this. From his early childhood, Abram questioned the faith of his father and embarked on a personal journey to find the truth. He came to believe that the entire universe was the work of a single Creator and began to teach this to others.

Jewish tradition claims that Abram tried to convince his father of the truth he discovered, to no avail. One day, left alone in his father's store, Abram took a hammer and smashed all the idols except the largest one and then placed the hammer in the hand of the last remaining idol. Upon his return, seeing the destruction, Abram's father asked him about the damage. Abram said, "The idols got into a fight, and the big one smashed all the other ones." Abram's father replied, "Don't be ridiculous! These idols have no life or power. They can't do anything." Abram replied, "Then why do you worship them?"[5]

This legend is not substantiated in any of the Jewish sacred writings. It is, however, indicative of Abram's character as the first Jewish patriarch to be highly esteemed for his obedience to the One True G-d. Belief in one G-d is a Jewish heritage that goes back to the very first man: Adam.

Belief that the Jews are G-d's chosen people rests on the covenant promise G-d made to them through Abram, whose name was later changed to Abraham (meaning "father of many").

The Jewish Origin of Creation

Judaism's perspective on the origin of all of creation—the universe and everything in this physical world, with humans of the highest living order—is drawn from the book of Genesis. However, according to Mike Shreve in his book *In Search of the True Light*, "Most Jews do not believe that Adam and Eve's transgression constituted the fall of the entire human race, nor do they believe in the serpent as [a being named] Satan [in disguise]. Concerning the nature of man, it's taught that man is a multifaceted unitary being. The first man, Adam, became a living soul when God breathed into him the breath of life. The soul/spirit of every human is believed to be created by God, whereas conception in the womb fashions the physical body. Man is a free agent able to choose between good and evil. Judaism does not believe, as Christianity does, that [since the first man and woman] mankind is born into this world under the burden of Original Sin. Rather, man's moral ambivalence stems from two inclinations within him: the good and the evil. The body and soul of man are valued as being in the image and likeness of God."[6]

The Promise for Deliverance

Genesis 1–3 gives the account of the origin of the universe, earth, and all life. G-d specifically instructed Adam and Eve not to eat of the Tree of the Knowledge of Good and Evil, warning that if they did, they would die. The embodiment of evil referred to as a serpent, appealing to human pride and lust, enticed the first man and woman, who then chose to disobey G-d. In response, G-d cursed the serpent to the ground and pronounced enmity between the serpent's seed (offspring) and the Seed of the woman. G-d revealed the pain and suffering Adam and Eve would experience as a result of their own free will choice to disobey. However, with the promise of enmity between the serpent's seed and the Seed of the woman, Jews believe G-d promised a future Deliverer who would redeem His people from exile—not from the penalty of sin as Christians believe. The Encyclopaedia Judaica offers a broader definition: it defines redemption as "salvation from the states or circumstances that destroy the value of human existence or human existence itself." Jews believe their Deliverer, or *Messiah,* which means Anointed One, will be associated with a specific series of events that have not yet occurred. These include the return of Jews to their homeland, the rebuilding of the Temple, and a Messianic Age of peace and understanding during which "the knowledge of G-d" fills the earth. Jews to this day are looking for the promised Deliverer.

Jewish Sacrificial System

In Genesis 3, once the first man, Adam, and the first woman, Eve, confessed their disobedience, G-d covered their naked bodies with tunics of animal skin. This instituted the first animal sacrifice for the covering of sin. Such sacrifices continued to be part of Jewish worship until the fall of the Jewish Temple in AD 70.

According to Genesis 12, the promise of a Deliverer was reiterated when the One True Creator that Abram worshiped blessed him and made a covenant promise to him. G-d directed Abram to leave his country, family, and father's house and go to a land that would be revealed to him. In exchange, G-d offered to make of Abram a great nation—one that would be a blessing for all the families of the earth. Abram accepted the covenant for himself and his family, and on behalf of the promised future nation. With this, according to some scholars, the Hebrew people were established in the estimated year of 1800 BC on the Gregorian calendar. On the Jewish calendar, which counts the years since creation, the date is estimated to be as early as 2001 to 2083 BC.[7]

At the age of seventy-five, in obedience to G-d, Abram adopted a nomadic lifestyle along with his wife Sarai, his family, and his household. He began traveling through land that is believed by Jews to include present-day Israel. When Abram came to Canaan, G-d appeared to him and pronounced that He would give this land to Abram's descendants. In commemoration of this promise, Abram built an altar. This is the land we call Israel today.

The Lineage of G-d's Chosen People

Years ensued, yet Abram bore no children from his wife Sarai. He inquired of G-d concerning the promise. G-d responded again that Abram's descendants would be too numerous to count and assured him that he would have an heir from his own body. Genesis 15 records that G-d made a covenant with Abram that his descendants would inherit the land from the river of Egypt to the great river Euphrates. With Abram as their forefather, Jews identify themselves as G-d's chosen people and rightful heirs of the land.

Sarai knew that she was well past childbearing years, so according to accepted custom of the day, she offered Hagar, her Egyptian maidservant, as a wife to Abram. Hagar conceived and bore Abram a son named Ishmael, who, according to Jewish, Muslim, and Christian tradition, is the ancestor of the Arabs. Abram was eighty-six years old when Ishmael was born.

When Abram was ninety-nine years old and still without any children from his wife Sarai, G-d appeared to him again, recorded in Genesis 17. G-d confirmed the covenant to Abram and his descendants as an everlasting covenant. G-d promised that Abram's descendants would be multiplied exceedingly. As a sign of the covenant, G-d instituted circumcision. This "mark" on the male reproductive organ was a perpetual reminder to the Jewish people that, whatever forces may work against them, G-d's people would multiply until they had reached their destiny.[8] It was at this time that G-d changed Abram's name to Abraham, which means the father of many nations, and changed Sarai's name to Sarah, which means princess.

A year later, when Abraham was one hundred and his wife was ninety, Sarah gave birth to a son, just as G-d promised. They obediently named their son Isaac.

Pamela Christian

The historical lineage from Isaac to Jacob (whose name was later changed to Israel) is recorded in the Jewish scriptures. The name Israel means "G-d strives," which conveys that G-d strives for His chosen people. The twelve sons of Jacob/Israel and his descendants ultimately comprised the twelve tribes of Israel. As generations passed, the tribes of Israel became slaves in Egypt, as foretold to Abram by G-d, recorded in Genesis 15. The Israelites suffered greatly under the pharaohs. The miraculous story of the Israelites' exodus under Moses, the prophet appointed by G-d for that time, is dramatic and an essential foundation to the Jewish faith. Discussion about the reality of the Exodus has a long history and continues to attract attention.

Escape from Slavery

The first five books of the Jewish scriptures provide history from creation by G-d, to man's rejection of G-d, culminating with man's deliverance from the bondage of slavery by G-d. Again, scholars disagree on dates and times, but generally agree as to the reality of the events themselves. However, there are some scholars who claim many of the events in the Torah to be figurative and not literal. Chapter endnotes are provided not only to substantiate what's written here, but to encourage you in your own personal study.

After hundreds of years of harsh slavery under Egyptian rule, G-d raised up a Jewish man named Moses to deliver His people. For this particular man to seek to deliver the Hebrews was most infuriating to the pharaoh named Ramses II. Through some amazing events recorded in Exodus 1 and 2, Moses was raised by the pharaoh's own sister as a part of the royal family—with all the education and luxuries of the Egyptian palace.

Moses' loyalty to the G-d of Israel drove him passionately to seek the deliverance of his people, whom he daily witnessed being abused and even slaughtered. The Torah describes a series of unspeakable disasters that fell upon the pharaoh and his kingdom: locust plagues, hailstorms, and, eventually, the mysterious death of the firstborn Egyptian children. The last tragedy convinces the reluctant pharaoh to let the Hebrew people go. This day is commemorated by Jews, to this day, as one of the most important festivals of the Jewish calendar known as *the Passover.*

In approximately 1496–1447 BC (some say 1290 BC), under G-d's guidance and power, Moses led the entire Hebrew people out of bondage and into freedom. Through the miraculous parting of the Red Sea, G-d had Moses lead His people across on dry ground to the land He had promised they would possess for their very own.[9]

The Jewish Law

An estimated 430 to 630 years after G-d's covenant promise for His people through Abraham, G-d presented Moses with His Law—also known as the Ten Commandments. For the first time in hundreds of years, the Hebrew people had freedom and they needed to know how to best live and prosper in their new-found lives. *The Law* was given by G-d to provide them instructions for living a life distinct from all others—demonstrating that they were a people chosen by G-d and were uniquely in His care. The specific Law, or *Ten Commandments,* can be found in Exodus 20:1–17. His miraculous care of providing them with daily food they did not gather is recorded in the book of Exodus 16.

Over time, Moses, perhaps with the assistance of Joshua, recorded all the Torah, which is identical to the first five books of the Christian Old Testament that exist today—also called by its Greek name, the Pentateuch. The five specific books are Genesis, Exodus, Leviticus, Numbers, and Deuteronomy. Jews also refer to these as the Books of

Moses. The word *Torah* means "to teach, or, instruction." The Torah contains 613 commandments, including the Ten Commandments, and provides the basis for nearly every aspect of Jewish life. It is the embodiment of the Jewish worldview and the foundation of the Jewish religion. Exodus, Leviticus, and Deuteronomy are devoted to identifying the specifics of Israel's constitution as determined by G-d—that is, G-d's instruction for His chosen people, regarding social welfare, criminal law, religious rituals, environmental policy, and more.

Jews refer to their entire scriptures as the *Tanakh*, which is actually an acronym for the texts of the Torah, Prophets, and Writings, which are the very same text of the Christian Old Testament. However, the sequence of books varies in comparison. Other sacred texts for Jews include the *Talmud* and *Midrash*, which provide the legal and narrative interpretations of the Torah as interpreted by Jewish religious leaders known as rabbis. All of these writings documenting their history, prophecy, poetry/worship, and instructions for living, revealing God's continual involvement, are essential to the Jewish identity.

After the Exodus

There were many prominent figures in the progression of Judaism during the years of the patriarchs. Following these years were the years of the kings—first for a united Israel, and then due to conflict a divided kingdom consisting of the regions of Judah (the northern territory) and Israel (the southern territory). Out of all the kings, not one is considered greater than King David. Beyond Israel, he is identified as one of the most prominent figures in the history of the world.

It's commonly believed that David was born in 1040 BC and lived as a young boy in Bethlehem. The youngest of seven brothers, he was identified as G-d's chosen one to be king of the Jews at a young age. In the book of First Samuel, G-d refers to David as a man after His own heart. Early in his life, he demonstrated strong allegiance to G-d, standing firm and courageous by G-d's power in major battles when mightier men failed. He became extraordinarily gifted with music and poetic genius and performed before the reigning King Saul.

As he grew, he proved to be a military success, an able general who conducted military campaigns with great success. He displayed unusual wisdom in the administration of government. His success in battle and popularity among the people roused jealousy in the heart of reigning King Saul. Though David would ultimately take the throne as G-d decreed, he spent many years running and hiding in fear of his life at the order of the vengeful King Saul.

Overall, David lived a life of contrasts. He was a great military conqueror, but he could not conquer himself. His life was a strange mixture of obedience and disobedience to G-d. No historical character more fully illustrates the moral range of human nature. The fact that the general trend of his life was eminently religious and spiritual, if not always consistent, together with his great genius and accomplishments, accounts for his very high place he occupies in Hebrew history. King David is ultimately heralded as the king who reunited the divided kingdom of Israel. David is one who proved G-d's faithfulness and gives hope to Jews and Christians alike. The scriptures reveal G-d as one who is quick to forgive and restore His people when they repent.[10]

From the pharaoh to the Holocaust to modern day events, the Jews, as G-d's chosen people, have endured unimaginable suffering where other peoples have perished entirely. History is a powerful tool that can help shape our world today in the light of truth.

Distinctions within Judaism

Peering back through history, there seems to be four different periods in the history of Judaism, each with its own religious distinction. The Early Years, 2000–500 BC, provided the foundational years where the fundamentals of the faith were developed. The next period is referred to as the Interim Years, 500 BC–AD 100, which was a period of infighting with various factions seeking prominence. Classical Judaism follows, in the years AD 100–1800, when finally one form took prominence and established the course for the bulk of Jewish history. This brings us to Modern Judaism, from AD 1800 to present.

The evolution of Modern Judaism presents us with four versions of the Jewish faith we see today: Orthodox, Conservative, Reform, and Reconstructionist, which respectively range from traditional to liberal to religiously progressive in their application of the *Tanakh*. The unification of the Jews is on the basis of their common connection to a set of sacred narratives expressing their relationship with G-d as a holy people. Judaism tends to emphasize practice over belief.[11]

Huston Smith, author of *The World's Religions: Our Great Wisdom Traditions* wrote, "What lifted the Jews from obscurity to permanent religious greatness was their passion for meaning. From the beginning to the end the Jewish quest for meaning was rooted in their understanding of God."[12] With a recognition that no one claims to be self-created and that human beings have specific limitations, the Jewish faith recognized the existence of the Creator of all things as self-existent, and therefore the One who imposes earthly limitations. The first lines of the first book of the Jewish Scriptures read, "In the beginning, G-d…"

The Jewish G-d

Judaism introduced a concept into human history that is revolutionary in all aspects, particularly in the aspect of morality and the notion of history in general—the idea of an infinite G-d who acts in history. The Jewish concept of G-d is that of Creator, Sustainer, and Supervisor—an infinite Being who is actively involved in all creation. To put it more philosophically: the entire physical world is a creation of G-d's consciousness. The universe has no independent existence outside of G-d "willing" it to exist.

Everything in the universe is under G-d's control—from the quantum to the cosmic. Jews believe that G-d knows and controls everything, making history a controlled process, not a series of random events, leading to a destination.

Beyond recognizing the existence of G-d, Jews have personified Him: "Where the Jews differed from their neighbors was not in envisioning God as personal, but in focusing its personalism in a single, supreme, nature-transcending will."[13] The Jewish view of G-d is that He is one in nature and He is the only G-d that exists. The G-d of Israel is in a category that differs from gods of other religions, not merely in degree, but in kind.[14] Their G-d is a G-d of righteousness, whose loving-kindness is from everlasting to everlasting and whose tender mercies are in all His works.

Beyond finding unique meaning in their G-d, Jews see great meaning in creation itself, in the human existence, in history, morality, justice, suffering, materialism, and in *Messianism*—which is the hope of G-d sending the Messiah (the Deliverer). The significant impact of the ancient Jews lies in the extent to which Western civilization has adopted their angle of vision on the deepest questions that life poses.

The Progression of Judaism

Early Judaism celebrated the Abrahamic covenant, followed by subsequent renewal of the convent that G-d made through the lineage of Abraham. In addition, their expressions of faith were made through various feasts and rituals and observance of the Torah—the Law, which was the Ten Commandments given by G-d to Moses for the Israeli people that guided them in all their worship and social conduct. The laws of western civilization, especially in America, are rooted in the laws of the Jews.

Though it is clear from Jewish scriptures that G-d intended the Israeli people to be a distinct bloodline, He accepted others who wanted to worship Him as their personal G-d (Genesis 17:27). Specific rites and rituals for expressions of worship were established by G-d and carried out by the people with the help of the appointed priests, ultimately in the Temple. Since the destruction of the Jerusalem Temple in AD 70, Temple worship, which included animal sacrifices for the covenant, has not been practiced.

The destruction of the Temple gave birth to Judaism as we know it today. Is Judaism a nationality, a race of people, a religion? It seems one could conclude that it's all three.

What follows in the next chapter is a look at Buddhism.

Chapter Six

Faith Findings—Buddhism

Buddhism is a religion that begins with a man called *the Buddha* who lived in India. His message during his later years caused people to seek him out to inquire what he was. Their inquiry was not concerning his name, origin, or ancestry, but to learn what order of being he belonged to. His answer gave title to himself and his message. Legend indicates when asked, "If you are not a god, an angel, or a saint, what are you?" Buddha's response was, "I am awake." From this, Buddha became known as the "Awakened One" or the "Enlightened One." Those who practice Buddhism seek to become awakened through their own spiritual journeys.

The Birth and Early Life of Buddha

The Buddha was born in roughly 563 BC in what is now Nepal, near the Indian border. His full name was Siddhartha Gautama of the Sakyas. He was born into royalty, lived in luxury, and was apparently extremely handsome. At sixteen, he married a neighboring princess, Yasodhara, who bore him a son.

Legend says that Gautama's father summoned fortunetellers to find out what the future held for his heir. Agreeing that he was no usual child, they stated that if Gautama remained in the world, he would unify India and become her greatest conqueror, or Universal King. If he forsook the world, he would become a world redeemer.

Determined to have his son become a worldly ruler like himself, Gautama's father surrounded him with all the pleasures of the senses, occupying him entirely with the delights of the world. The king provided the young prince with different palaces for each of the seasons, with musicians, dancers, and beautiful companions to entertain him. The king did everything within his power to banish all unpleasantness from Gautama's life.

Despite these enormous efforts, according to legend of "the Four Passing Sites," Gautama came into contact with the ugly realities of life. Legend says that at age twenty-nine, Gautama decided to leave the palace grounds and explore the life of the city around him. His father, the king, worried that his son might encounter something disturbing and thus begin to question his life of luxury, so he ordered all unpleasant sights removed. He had the buildings freshly painted, flowers and incense placed all about, and everyone who was suffering hidden away.

It is said that heavenly messengers (some sort of celestial beings) appeared to Gautama as he rode throughout the city. The first of these messengers appeared as an old person stricken with infirmities. The second messenger appeared as a person suffering greatly with disease. The third appeared as a corpse. The prince was startled at each encounter because in his protected young life he'd never come into contact with old age, sickness, or death. He questioned his charioteer about what he was seeing and asked if everyone was subject to this fate. The charioteer replied that all who are born will grow older, experience sickness, and die.

On the fourth occasion, the last of the heavenly encounters appeared in the form of a monk. Gautama questioned his charioteer again, who explained that this was someone who had renounced the world in order to seek enlightenment and liberation. These encounters, according to legend, so moved him that his interest in worldly pursuits ended and his entire focus turned to seek *enlightenment* (truth and wisdom) and *liberation* (the cessation of the perpetual cycle of reincarnation).[1]

In his late twenties, he decided to depart from his wife and son and life in his palace to follow the call of a truth-seeker. He first sought the two foremost Hindu masters of the day to gain their wisdom and learn from their vast tradition. He learned a great deal about *raga yoga* and Hindu philosophy, ultimately finding criticism with much of it. He then concluded that he had learned all these *yogis* could teach him. He turned to a life of *asceticism*, believing that his body was holding him back. He joined a group of ascetics and proved himself to be a man of enormous willpower, outdoing his associates in every austerity they proposed. In the end, he grew so weak and faint that had it not been for the maiden Sujata tending him by feeding him some warm rice and gruel, Gautama could have easily died.[2]

These two experiences provided Gautama with the first constructive plank for his program, the principle of the Middle Way between the extremes of asceticism and indulgence. He chose the concept of the *rationed life,* where the body is given what it needs to function optimally, but no more. Gautama devoted the final phase of his quest to a combination of rigorous thought and mystic concentration along the lines of *raja yoga.*

The legend continues with a single occasion where Gautama, determined to experience a breakthrough, sat down under a Bo Tree (short for *bodhi,* or enlightenment). Buddhist tradition believes this was an epic-making evening when Gautama vowed not to arise until enlightenment was his. The Evil One, not wanting Gautama to succeed, rushed to the scene to disrupt his concentrations. The Evil One used Kama, the God of Desire, and Mara, the Lord of Death. Kama paraded three voluptuous women before him, but Gautama was not tempted. Mara assailed the aspirant with hurricanes, torrential rains, and showers of flaming rocks. But Gautama had so emptied himself of his finite self that the weapons turned into flower petals when they entered his concentration. With a final desperate attempt, Mara challenged Gautama's right to do what he was doing. In response, Gautama touched the earth with his fingertip and the earth responded with hundred-fold thundering roars, "I bear you witness." The Evil One fled and the "gods of heaven" descended upon Gautama in rapture, bestowing upon him victory garlands and perfumes. With this, he was miraculously restored with the euphoria of "true being" the Great Awakening had arrived. Gautama's being was transformed and he emerged as the Buddha.[3]

The tradition of the legend states that all of creation responded, filling the morning air with rejoicing, the earth quaked six ways with wonder, and ten thousand galaxies shuddered in awe as lotuses bloomed on every tree, thus turning the entire universe into a bouquet of flowers whirling through the air. In this utterly blissful environment, Buddha remained for seven full days. He tried to arise on the eighth day but was again overwhelmed by bliss. For a total of forty-nine days, he was caught up in rapture after which his "glorious glance" opened onto the world.[4]

Mara, lying in wait, with one last temptation, appealed to what had always been Gautama's strongest point—his reason. Basically, Mara challenged Gautama with the notion that there would be no way he could communicate or relay the truth that he'd experienced to others—no one else would be able to understand. So why not be done with the body and just enjoy this Nirvana (bliss) for yourself? Mara was so persuasive that he nearly convinced Gautama, but ultimately Gautama answered, "There will be some who will understand," and with that, Mara was banished from Buddha forever.[5]

What is curious about this legend is that Buddha did not personally believe in the divine, which presumably would apply to the Evil One, Kama, and Mara.

Buddha's Later Years

Following, Buddha's life was that of wandering India, preaching his ego-shattering, life-redeeming message. He founded an order of monks and nuns which he diligently trained, teaching them to challenge the deadness of Brahmin society. This brought upon him resentment and bewilderment from his fellow countrymen. Undaunted, he maintained a rigorous public preaching schedule in addition to offering private counseling. People sought him out, even from distant countries, all of whom were welcome. To withstand the relentless pressures and demands, he patterned his life following a rigid schedule of work and withdrawal.

After a ministry life of nearly forty-nine years, his hair white and his body weak, at the age of eighty, the Buddha died. This was around 483 BC. Legend tells he'd eaten a meal with a disciple that resulted in dysentery. Lore is that his concern for others was great even on his deathbed. To comfort the disciple who served him and might feel responsible, Buddha stated that of all the meals he'd ever eaten, two stood out—the one that made it possible for him to regain his strength and start his quest for true enlightenment, and this last one that opened the final way to Nirvana.

If legend is correct, Gautama was indeed no ordinary child, and neither was he a common man. But he was a mortal man who lived and died and had a profound impact on countless people throughout history—even being referred to as "wisdom personified." His religion has become known as one of infinite compassion: "His self-giving so impressed his biographers that they could explain it only in terms of a momentum that had acquired its trajectory in the animal stages of his incarnations."[6]

Buddha's popularity grew so great, as did the size of his order, that kings sought him out and bowed before him. There was great pressure to turn him into a God, but the Buddha rebuffed all this categorically, insisting that he was human in every respect.

He realized that his mission in life was to promote good and happiness in the lives of others. He accepted his mission with no regard for his own personal cost, and this won the hearts and minds of India. "The monk Gautama has gone forth into the religious life, giving up the great clan of his relatives, giving up much money and gold, treasure both buried and above ground. Truly, while he was still a young man without gray hair on his head, in the beauty of his early manhood, he went forth from the luxurious household life into the homeless state."[7]

The Origin of Buddhism and Creation

Buddhism is a religion that began by rejecting Hinduism. In time, Hinduism came to accept some of the Buddha's teachings as reforms for their own belief structure. But ultimately, the philosophies and structures were again made distinct. Buddhists can be found in every Asian country except India, though today some are reappearing there.

Buddha introduced a renewed emphasis on kindness to all living things, non-killing of animals, elimination of the caste system, and the strong emphasis on ethics in general. Buddhism does not include belief in an Almighty God. In Buddhism, there is no faith owed to a supernatural being. Buddhists believe that *Dharma* (the teachings in Buddhism) exist, regardless if there is a Sakyamuni Buddha (a literal Buddha), and they do not ascribe to him deity as some Hindus do. Especially emphasized in Mahayana Buddhism, all sentient beings (that go beyond human beings) have Buddha Nature/Essence. One can become a Buddha (a supreme enlightened being) in due course if one practices diligently and attains purity of mind (i.e., absolutely no delusions of afflictions). The doctrine of *Sunyata,* or Emptiness, is unique to Buddhism. This doctrine asserts the transcendental nature of Ultimate Reality. Buddhists believe in six different realms of existence, three graduated desirable realms and three graduated undesirable realms, that are constantly visited based on *karma* until a sentient being attains Nirvana (i.e. virtual exhaustion of karma, habitual traces, defilements, and delusions.

In Buddhism, the ultimate objective of followers is enlightenment and/or liberation from *Samsara* (the perpetual wandering on the wheel of *reincarnation*). This perpetual wandering is determined by karma, though karma in Buddhism is considered a bit differently than in Hinduism.

Buddhism does not address the origin of humanity. The very idea that there could be a beginning to the world, let alone mankind, is questionable to most Buddhists. In Buddhist literature, the belief in a creator God is frequently mentioned and rejected. Belief in a God is utterly contrary to Buddhism's fundamental position that karma determines destiny. Even contemplation regarding the matter of God, the origin of the world, and similar questions would result in bad karma according to Buddha.

Followers of Buddha see him as their incomparable guide on their own path of purity. According to Buddhism, success on this path places heavy emphasis on self-reliance, self-discipline, and individual striving to liberate oneself, using meditation (seeking altered levels of consciousness considered essential for success), which in the end is to become completely free from self.

The Teachings of Buddha

Buddha's teachings stemmed from what he called the *Four Noble Truths.* The first is that life is *dukkha,* usually translated as "suffering," but that's not entirely accurate. A better understanding of *dukkha* is needed to adequately comprehend his teachings. India's thought supports the basic premise that fundamentally everything is well, and therefore, optimism is intact. But the Buddha saw clearly that life, as typically lived, is unfulfilling and replete with insecurity. The second Noble Truth is *tanha. Tanha* seeks to identify the origin of life's suffering that Buddha taught was found in desire (the translation of *tanah*), in the sense of self-serving desires. The third Noble Truth is overcoming selfish craving. The fourth Noble Truth is the end of suffering, which he taught is accomplished on an Eightfold Path.

Karma in Buddhism is not quite the same as in Hinduism. Buddha taught that karma occurs from willful action. A morally good action will produce good karma and a morally bad action will generate bad karma. However, don't conclude that Buddha then taught that good deeds are what people should focus on, because even good things eventually change—beauty fades, pleasure dissipates, joy passes, and ultimately tragedy is experienced. Matters of life, according to Buddha, are simply a long progression of arising and digressing experiences that creates the cycle from which people must seek to be freed. Karma produces *reincarnation,* which brings another cycle of the painful aspects of life. A person is trapped in a continuous cycle of death, life, and rebirth all because of karma that is generated when acting out of desire.

The Buddhist's journey is experienced in four stages, each with its own measure of Nirvana:

1. The "Stream-Entrant," or novice who only catches a glimpse of Nirvana.
2. The "Once-Returner," or one destined to be reincarnated only one time before experiencing full Nirvana.
3. The "Never-Returner," or one who has an even deeper knowledge of Nirvana and is assured that he or she will not be reincarnated.
4. The "Worthy One," or *Arhat*, who is totally pure and completely free from desire.[8]

The Eightfold Path or habits that are to specifically direct the Buddhist's way of life are expressions of three essential categories for living:

1. Wisdom—two of the eight fall in this category intended to increase one's appreciation for truth. They are "right understanding" and "right intent/aim."
2. Ethical conduct—the three habits in this category promote the Buddhist lifestyle in the effort to remove desire. These are "right speech," "right action," and "right livelihood."
3. Mental discipline—the remaining three are mental exercises to aid in cultivating one's way through life. The last are "right effort," "right mindfulness," and "right concentration."[9]

The perfected Buddha, called an *Arhat*, is one who has freed him/herself from the idea of self and is therefore able to live in this world without any desires or cravings. Without craving, action accumulates no karma. Without karma, there is no rebirth and one then enters Nirvana. Nirvana is not a heavenly place. Nirvana is the final beatitude that transcends suffering, karma, and *samsara*. It is sought especially in Buddhism through the extinction of desire and individual consciousness. It is the extinguishment of all desire, or the realization that the self does not really exist and human desire is therefore meaningless, and a return to the source from which one originally came.

Those who consider themselves Buddhists insist that their way is a practical way of living in the world just as much as it is a comprehensive way of thinking about the world. By way of detachment from the world and even the self, one can be free from the pain of suffering.

Distinctions within Buddhism

While only 0.5 percent of Americans are Buddhists, they are divided along lines of national origin, ethnicity, education, class, and sectarian affiliation. There is no one form of Buddhism in the United States. Rather, a plurality of different forms of Buddhism exist that for the most part keep to themselves and have only recently begun to interact.[10]

There are two main sects of this faith—*Theravada Buddhism* (School of the Elders) and *Mahayana Buddhism* (Great Vehicle). While all who practice Buddhism agree that the Four Noble Truths and the Eightfold Path are essential to the faith, there are distinctions concerning other matters.

Theravada is traditionally described as Classical Buddhism, which historians, for the most part, see to be the closest to what Siddhartha Gautama and his first disciples would have practiced. Mahayana Buddhism is the term for a variety of Buddhist groups with certain beliefs and practices in common that are believed to have been developed sometime between 100 BC and AD 100, about four to five hundred years after Siddhartha Gautama's death. Theravada Buddhism honors Siddhartha Gautama as the ideal man.

Mahayana Buddhism teaches that Siddhartha Gautama was an incarnation of a celestial, heavenly Buddha who exists throughout time. Mahayana Buddhists see Buddha as a divine figure able to assist the faithful in their pursuit of enlightenment,[11] which is inconsistent with what Buddha said about himself and about the existence of the divine.

Americans' Embrace of Buddhism

Many Americans embracing Buddhism see it as a means to detach, maintain neutrality, and find peace in a world of injustice and suffering. The attraction to Buddhism is largely the same as for Americans to Hinduism. However, Buddhism offers the additional attraction of overcoming debasing human characteristics.

A writer of an Internet blog and a website entitled Buddhist Answers offers this: the open spirit of investigation and discovery in *dharma* practice is known as the *Kalama Sutta.* This sutra is named after the Kalamas, a village people who had asked the Buddha how they could know which among the many different religious teachings to believe. The Buddha said that they should not blindly believe anyone—not their parents or teachers, not the books or transitions, not even the Buddha himself. Rather, they should look carefully into their own experience to see those actions that lead to more greed, more hatred, more delusion and abandon them; and they should look to see what things lead to greater love, generosity, wisdom, and peace and cultivate these.[12]

When Bhikkhu Bodhi of the Bodhi Monastery in United States was questioned on his opinion as to why Buddhism was becoming so popular in the United States, he replied, "It is not difficult to understand why Buddhism should appeal to Americans at this particular junction of our history. Theistic religions have lost their hold on the minds of many educated Americans and this has opened up a deep spiritual vacuum that needs to be filled. For many, materialistic values are profoundly unsatisfying, and Buddhism offers a spiritual teaching that fits the bill. It is rational, experiential, practical, and personally verifiable. It brings concrete benefits that can be realized in one's own life; it propounds lofty ethics and an intellectually cogent philosophy. Also less auspiciously, it has an exotic air that attracts those fascinated by the mystical and esoteric."[13]

To continue in the effort to learn the orgins and basic teachings of the major world religions, the next chapter deals with Hinduism, often referred to as the oldest religion in the world.

Chapter Seven

Faith Findings—Hinduism

*H*induism is an ancient religious practice with no founder or known date of origin. It is a collection of traditions and philosophies that have been developed over thousands of years. What Westerners call Hinduism, Indians call *sanatana dharma*. Some scholars identify Hinduism as the oldest religion.

The History of Hinduism

The term *Hinduism* simply derives from the word *India*. Hinduism may have been coined from the Persian word Hindu, meaning *river*, used to describe the people of the Indus River Valley. Hinduism includes numerous traditions and philosophies that have been developed over thousands of years. These are closely related and share common themes, but they do not constitute a unified set of beliefs or practices. Hinduism is not a homogeneous, organized system. Its diversity makes generalizing the religion a challenge.

Nomadic Aryan tribes, originally from Persia, settled in India, bringing their religion known as *Vedism* with them. Vedism could be called the first layer of Hinduism that was developed over a long history of reflection and revision and additions. A look at the three basic historical periods in Indian history, each with its own set of sacred writings, helps to explain the development process.

During 1500–500 BC the prominent sacred writings were the *Vedas*. These were not codified until about 600 BC. During 1000–300 BC, writings called the *Upanishads* were introduced with the Smriti writings last entering the scene last around 500 BC–AD 300.

Hindus themselves refer to their religion as *sanatana dharma*, "eternal religion," and as *varnasrama dharma*, a word emphasizing the fulfillment of duties (*dharma*) appropriate to one's class (*varna*) and stage of life (*asrama*).

The Gods and Writings of Hinduism

While there are innumerable sects, most Hindus worship one or more deities, believe in reincarnation, value the practice of meditation, and observe festive holidays like Diwali and Holi.[1]

For most Hindus, fundamental belief include the authority of the *Vedas* (the oldest Indian sacred texts also referred to as *Shruti*) and the *Brahmans* (writings of the priests). These sacred texts differentiate the faith from Buddhism and Jainism. However, some Hindus reject one of both of these authorities too.

The word *Veda* means knowledge. The *Vedas* are considered to be sacred, revealed knowledge that is eternal and that God brings out at the beginning of each creation cycle. The *Vedas* are meant to protect *dharma* (religion) and protect cosmic order (*Rtam*).

The authors and dates of most Hindu sacred texts are unknown. Additional sacred texts include the *Aranyakas*, the *Upanishads*, *Brahmans*, the *Epics*, the *Purana*, and the *Bhagavad Gita*, to name but a few. The *Bhagavad Gita* is considered to be revered scripture by most Hindus today, and it holds an ambiguous position between the *Upanishads* of the *Vedas* and the *Epics*.

Many Hindus are devoted followers of Shiva or Vishnu, whom they regard as the only true God. Others look inward to the divine self (*atman*). However, most recognize the existence of *Brahman*, the unifying principle and Supreme Reality behind all that exists. Note that a specific belief about God or gods is not considered one of the essentials. This is a major difference between Hinduism and strictly monotheistic religions like Christianity, Judaism, and Islam.

The Hindu View of Humanity

The Hindu concept of human nature and destiny believes that individual human souls (*jivas*) enter the world mysteriously by the power of Brahman (Brahman is the collective spirit-soul essence of the universe). Questions regarding how or for what reasons are not fully explained. Souls make their way through the universe until they break free into the limitless atmosphere of illumination, which is *liberation*. They begin as souls of the simplest forms of life, but do not vanish upon death. Rather, the soul returns to a higher or lower bodily form until ultimately a human body is attained. This process of passing through a sequence of bodies is known as *reincarnation* or transmigration of the soul in an endless passage through cycles of life, death and rebirth. "the Law of Karma" is the mechanism that promotes the soul. The literal meaning of karma is work, but as a doctrine, it roughly means the moral law of cause and effect.[2]

Through efforts believed to promote good karma, a Hindu's goal is to become free from continuous wheel of reincarnations. According to their beliefs, there are three ways to do this: (1) being devoted to any of the Hindu gods or goddesses, (2) through meditation that includes psychophysical exercises acknowledging life as an illusion with Brahman the only real thing, and (3) dedicating one's self to various religious works. For Hindus of a devotional focus, release from the cycle means being in the presence of god(s). Those of a philosophical persuasion look forward to uniting with their original source, such as a drop of rain merging with the sea. The ultimate goal for a Hindu is to work through life in this world in order to come back as something better the next time, or better yet, to escape the need to come back at all.

The Teachings of Hinduism

In Hinduism, there are four purposes of human life: *Dharma* (fulfilling one's purpose), *Artha* (prosperity), *Kama* (desire, sexuality, and enjoyment), and *Moksha* (enlightenment). The premise of Hinduism is to find fulfillment in what people really want. According to Hindu belief, this is to have infinite being, infinite knowledge, and infinite bliss. This is attained as one seeks higher states of being in an effort to release the god within (*atman*). Hinduism says its purpose is to pass beyond imperfection altogether by working to overcome the strictures in the human existence that separate us from perfection. This is accomplished through denying personal ego (self-worship), acquiring transcendent knowledge, and pressing beyond our restricted being. If a Hindu fails to reach selfless perfection in this life, he believes he will continue to return to the earth repeatedly until he does.

Hindus believe in a *caste system,* which is a special system of class order. They believe that Brahma (a god) created Manu. Manu was the first man and from him, according to Brahma's plan, four different types of people emerged. Out of Manu's head came the *Brahmins,* the best and most holy people who comprise the priestly class. Out of Manu's hands came the *Kshatriyas,* the rulers and warriors. The *craftsmen* came from Manu's thighs and are called *Vaisyas.* From Manu's feet came the people known as *Sudras.* Therefore, they believe that the structure of the caste system is divinely inspired.[3] Additionally, there is a casteless group of people known as the *Untouchables.*

For Hindus the only truth is *Brahman*. This is the infinite supreme universal spirit-soul that is all-prevailing. The entire visualized world is a tiny part of the same. They believe that what we see or feel with our senses in this world is Divine Illusion or *Maya* and is therefore untrue. Hindus sometimes refer to Brahman as the Absolute Godhead and they believe that each person is a small part of Brahman. Hindus worship three hundred thousand different reincarnations of Brahman. For most Hindus there are three major gods—Brahma (Creator), Vishnu (Preserver), and Shiva (Destroyer)—and three major goddesses—Saraswati (Knowledge), Lakshmi (Wealth), and Parvati or Shakti (Power).

Hinduism is not so much a religion as it is a collection of ten thousand or more religions that intermingle. Hinduism has no limits. One can be an atheist, believe in a personal god, or believe that everything in this world is an illusion and still be a good Hindu. This is because the Hindu heart loves the all-embracing approach.[4]

The American Attraction to Hinduism

In the twentieth century, Hinduism began to gain popularity in the West. Its different worldview and its tolerance for diversity in belief made it an attractive alternative to traditional Western religion. The appeal of Hinduism to modern Western culture is not difficult to comprehend:

- Hinduism is comfortable with evolutionary thinking. As modern science emphasizes our physical evolution, Hinduism emphasizes our spiritual evolution.
- Modern psychology and sociology emphasizes the basic goodness and unlimited potential of human nature. Hinduism emphasizes man's essential divinity.

- Modern philosophy emphasizes the relativity of all truth claims. Hinduism tolerates many seemingly contradictory religious beliefs.

- Hinduism emphasizes the primacy of the spiritual over material reality. Hinduism appeals to many that have become disillusioned with strictly material pursuits.[5]

The vast majority of American Hindus are Indian immigrants who began arriving in great numbers after 1965, when immigration laws were loosened. Most now reside in high concentrations around large cities such as Los Angeles, New York City, Houston, Washington, and Chicago.[6]

About 80 percent of India's population regard themselves as Hindus. It's estimated that around thirty million who consider themselves Hindu live outside India. Based on the US State Department's International Religious Freedom Report 2006, the US Hindu population is about 1.2 million—a tiny fraction of the 900 million Hindus worldwide. This, however, reveals that the acceptance of Hinduism is increasing since the 1995 estimate that reported 800 million Hindus worldwide. "The history of Hinduism in America is still being written," said Diana Eck, a Harvard University professor of comparative religion and Indian studies. The influence of Hinduism on Americans is increasing. More Americans (estimates run into the millions) have incorporated elements of Hinduism such as meditation and yoga into their lives as a spiritual supplement or to help relieve stress. "Most of those who embrace these Hindu practices consider themselves Christians or Jews and wouldn't dream of calling themselves Hindus," Eck said.[7]

Hindu thought has influenced the West indirectly by way of religious movements including Hare Krishna, the philosophy of the New Age movement, and others. There are scores of modern religious cults and sects which Hinduism has influenced in varying degrees.

Millions of Americans have taken up Hindu practices such as meditation, developing altered states of consciousness, asceticism, and seeking "enlightenment" through the incorporation of the chakra system, and yoga, along with seminars on health and spirituality—most notably New Age.[8]

In the next chapter, we'll learn more about the New Age movement and its teachings.

Chapter Eight

Faith Findings—Secular

An estimated 1.1 billion people claim that their beliefs fall into the category of *secular humanism* or *non-religious*. For the purposes of this book, secular humanism or non-religious includes *New Age, atheism,* and *agnosticism*. Because of the large number of people who identify with these, discussing this category is necessary.

The Founding of New Age

New Age, also referred to as New Age Christianity, is a worldview that was channeled through Helen Schucman, a professor of medical psychology with Columbia University. She claimed that one day in 1965, she heard an inner voice that instructed her, stating, "This is a course in miracles. Please take notes." Over a seven-year period of time, she took notes. Then in 1975, her notes were published, entitled *A Course in Miracles,* by the Foundation for Inner Peace and its related organization, the Foundation for a Course in Miracles. Initially, the course was received as something of an underground classic for New Age seekers who studied it individually or in small groups.[1]

The Teachings of New Age

The course is described as a self-study program of spiritual psychotherapy contained in three books. It is not a religion, but rather a psychological mind training based on universal spiritual themes. The practical goal of the course is the attainment of inner peace through the practice of forgiveness. It's an educational program that is spiritual in nature, rather than religious, for retraining the mind. Although Christian terminology is used along with references from just about every other world religion, the course expresses a universal experience.[2]

Described by many as "New Age Christianity," it posits a Jesus who offers more love and forgiveness (in contrast to *what they understand* about the Christian Jesus), while wanting less suffering, sacrifice, separating, and sacrament to help humanity work through troubled times. This belief system claims there is no sin, no evil, and no devil, and that God is "in" everyone and everything. The main purpose is to teach people to rethink everything they believe about God and life. The Course Workbook reveals it is a course in mind training and is dedicated to thought reversal.[3] Some have noted that the concepts contained in the course are primarily a hodgepodge of teachings from various world religions.

The Expansion of New Age

Schucman died in 1981, but the popularity of the course didn't wane. Marianne Williamson's appearance on a 1992 *Oprah Winfrey Show* with Oprah's promotion of Williamson's book, *A Return to Love: Reflections on the Principles of A Course in Miracles*, greatly increased America's focus on New Age concepts. The appearance also propelled Williamson's book to the top of the *New York Times* bestseller list. This launched a radio show opportunity on Oprah Winfrey's X Satellite in January 2008, in which Williamson began to teach the New Age philosophy.

Williamson is one of today's premier New Age leaders, along with Neale Donald Walsch, author of *Conversations with God*. Walsch also co-founded the American Renaissance Alliance in 1997. This organization later became the Global Renaissance Alliance of New Age leaders and changed names again in 2005 to the Peace Alliance. This group seeks to usher in an era of global peace founded on the principles of a New Age/New Spirituality that they refer to as a "civil rights movement for the soul." They agree that the principles of this New Age/New Spirituality are clearly articulated in *A Course in Miracles*—which is fast becoming the New Age bible.[4]

Gaz Parker is one among many former followers who extend much caution concerning New Age beliefs. What he writes on his blog may seem like outlandish fringe thought at first read, but considering his experience in addition to the testimonies of many others, it is prudent to include his warning: "The New Age is a vast topic and both Helen Schucman and William Thetford [scribal colleague of Schucman's *A Course in Miracles*] along with Oprah's luciferic church are just tiny components to a much larger and sinister satanic plan. The New Age movement is a road map to bringing in a one-world satanic system under the guise of a heaven on earth scenario. The topic is nothing new; there have been countless occult revivals throughout history. It is certainly something that should not be treated lightly—only covering the surface is deceptive and potentially dangerous. This is why I started my blog—to expose the deeper roots of the New Age movement."

With this blunt explanation and the growing numbers of people attracted to this belief system, it behooves anyone attracted to New Age to learn more than this book intends to cover. You will find Gaz's blog at http://www.newagedeception.net.

The Secular Humanist View

The Council for Secular Humanism is claimed to be America's leading organization for non-religious people. They purport that for many, mere atheism or agnosticism are insufficient and incomplete. Additionally, they note that atheism and agnosticism are silent on larger questions of values and meaning. According to the Council for Secular Humanism, "If Meaning in life is not ordained from on high, what small-m meanings can we work out among our selves? If eternal life is an illusion, how can we make the most of our only lives? As social beings sharing a godless world, how should we coexist? For the questions that remain unanswered after we've cleared our minds of gods and souls and spirits, many atheists, agnostics, skeptics, and freethinkers turn to secular humanism. Secular humanists claim that far from living in a moral vacuum, they wish to encourage wherever possible the growth of moral awareness."[5]

The Teachings of Secular Humanism

The Council for Secular Humanism explains that secular humanists believe human values should express a commitment to improve human welfare in this world. Human welfare is understood in the context of our interdependence upon the environment and other living things. Ethical principles should be evaluated by their consequences for people, not by how well they conform to preconceived ideas of right and wrong.

Secular humanism denies that meaning, values, and ethics are imposed from a higher being. In essence, this is a simple form of atheism, but secular humanism goes farther, challenging humans to develop their own values. Secular humanism maintains that through a process of value inquiry, reflective men and women can reach rough agreement concerning values, and craft ethical systems that deliver desirable results under most circumstances.

Moreover, secular humanists suggest the basic components of effective morality are universally recognized. Paul Kurtz also wrote about the "common moral decencies" which are qualities including integrity, trustworthiness, benevolence, and fairness. These qualities are celebrated by almost every human religion, not because God ordained them, according to their thinking, but because human beings cannot thrive in communities where these values are ignored.

According to the Council for Secular Humanism, "Secular humanism offers a nonreligious template that may one day guide much of humanity in pursuing fulfilling and humane lives—lives that are rich intellectually, ethically, and emotionally, without reliance on religious faith." Tantamount to their beliefs is a commitment to democracy which excludes all varieties of belief that seek supernatural sanction for their values or espouse rule by dictatorship. "Democratic secular humanism has creatively flowered in modern times with the growth of freedom and democracy. Countless millions of thoughtful persons have espoused secular humanist ideals, have lived significant lives, and have contributed to the building of a more humane and democratic world. The modern secular humanist outlook has led to the application of science and technology to the improvement of the human condition. This has had a positive effect on reducing poverty, suffering, and disease in various parts of the world, in extending longevity, on improving transportation and communication, and in making the good life possible for more and more people. It has led to the emancipation of hundreds of millions of people from the exercise of blind faith and fears of superstition and has contributed to their education and the enrichment of their lives."[6]

The Expansion of Secular Humanism

The council also states on their website that they campaign for a more secular and ethical society. The council presents the case for understanding the world without reference to a God, working to separate church and state, and defend the rights of those who reject religious beliefs.

A primary concept in their beliefs is "free inquiry." The council opposes any tyranny over the mind of man, any efforts by ecclesiastical, political, ideological, or social institutions to shackle free thought. They claim churches and states impose tyrannies as an attempt to enforce the edicts of religious bigots. Furthermore, they believe that free inquiry has been censored to impose orthodoxy on beliefs and values and to control heretics and unbelievers.

As result, according to the council's Declaration, this organization works to prevent any religious group from influencing government. "The lessons of history are clear: wherever one religion or ideology is established and given a dominant position in the state, minority opinions are in jeopardy. A pluralistic, open democratic society allows all points of view to be heard. Any effort to impose an exclusive conception of Truth, Piety, Virtue, or Justice upon the whole of society is a violation of free inquiry."[7]

Local groups representing the Council for Secular Humanism have existed in each state of the United States and Canada that meet to explore ideas and encourage one another in their beliefs. They've held regular regional and national conferences, and the Council for Secular Humanism boasts affiliation with the Secular Coalition for America, which represents secular Americans in our nation's capital. The Secular Coalition for America claims that sectarian *ideologies* are the new *theologies* political parties and governments use in their mission to crush dissident opinion.[8]

The Core Viewpoint of Secular Humanism

One of the core viewpoints of secular humanists is in the concept of *evolution*. Crediting the existence of everything created to evolution, coupled with the belief that religion or matters of faith should not influence government, is central to the council.

Evolution is accepted as the answer for the secular believers of origin—how did we get here? They believe that evolution is supported by science whereas creation is a theory that man has concocted. This aligns with the council's Declaration, which states:

> The evolution of the species is supported so strongly by the weight of evidence that it is difficult to reject it. Accordingly, we deplore the efforts by fundamentalists (especially in the United States) to invade the science classrooms, requiring that creationist theory be taught to students and requiring that it be included in biology textbooks. This is a serious threat both to academic freedom and to the integrity of the educational process. We believe that creationists surely should have the freedom to express their viewpoint in society. Moreover, we do not deny the value of examining theories of creation in educational courses on religion and the history of ideas; but it is a sham to mask an article of religious faith as a scientific truth and to inflict that doctrine on the scientific curriculum. If successful, creationists may seriously undermine the credibility of science itself.[9]

Addressing concern for the science classrooms, the council's Declaration espouses that mass media today is viewed as the primary institutions of public information and education, increasingly replacing the schools. Although the electronic media provide unparalleled opportunities for extending cultural enrichment and enjoyment and powerful learning opportunities, there has been a serious misdirection of their purposes. In totalitarian societies, the media serve as the vehicle of propaganda and indoctrination. Television, radio, films, and mass publishing in democratic societies too often cater to the lowest common denominator and have become banal wastelands. The fact that the media (particularly in the United States, in the opinion of secularists) are inordinately dominated by a pro-religious bias is of special concern. "The views of preachers, faith healers, and religious hucksters go largely unchallenged, and the secular outlook is not given an opportunity for a fair hearing. We believe that television directors and producers have an obligation to redress the balance and revise their programming. Indeed, there is a broader task that all those who believe in democratic secular humanist values will recognize, namely, the need to embark upon a long term program of public education and enlightenment concerning the relevance of the secular outlook to the human condition."[10]

Islam, the second largest religion in the world, is the topic of the next chapter.

Chapter Nine

Faith Findings—Islam

As you will gather from the information in this chapter, *Islam* is more than a religious belief. Islam is a way of life: religiously, governmentally, politically, socially, and culturally.

The word *Islam* is derived from the Arabic root *slm*, which primarily means *peace*, with the secondary meaning of *surrender*. The complete literal meaning is "the peace that comes when one's life is surrendered to *Allah*," which is the Islamic name for God. Muslims explain that Islam originated with Allah as revealed in their sacred writings known as the Koran. The word Allah comes from joining two words, *the* and *God*. Islam is a monotheistic religion, which is belief that there is only one God. Those who adhere to Islam are known as *Muslims*.

The Muslim View of God and Creation

Modern-day Muslims believe that Allah created all that exists. Some of the beliefs parallel those of Judaism and Christianity. First, they believe that Allah created the world and then He created man. As the Jewish scriptures and the Christian Bible account, Adam was the first man created. The descendants of Adam included Noah, Shem, and Abraham. Abraham married Sarah, who was unable to bear him a child. Sarah then offered her maidservant, Hagar, to Abraham for his second wife. Hagar conceived and bore a son who was named Ishmael. Some years later, Sarah conceived and she bore a son named Isaac. Because of the contentiousness between the two women, Sarah demanded that Abraham banish Hagar from the tribe family. At this point, the similarity between Judaism, Christianity, and Islam departs. Muslims believe, according to the Koran, that Ishmael left and settled in Mecca, and that his descendants flourished in Arabia, ultimately becoming Muslims.

Mecca sits in a barren hollow between two ranges of steep hills in the west of present-day Saudi Arabia. To its immediate west lies the Red Sea coast; to the east stretches the great Rub'Al-Khali or Empty Quarter, which is the largest continuous body of sand on earth.

Islam's Origin

Classic Islamic tradition tells the story about the religion's founding. In the centuries leading up to the arrival of Islam, Mecca was a local pagan sanctuary of considerable antiquity. Religious rituals revolved around the *Ka'ba*—a shrine, still central in Islam today. Muslims believe the Ka'ba was originally built by Ibrahim (known to Christians and Jews as Abraham) and his son Isma'il (Ishmael). As Mecca became increasingly prosperous in the sixth century AD, pagan idols of varying sizes and shapes multiplied rapidly. By the early seventh century, a pantheon of some 360 statues and icons surrounded the Ka'ba, inside of which were found renderings of Jesus and the Virgin Mary, among other idols.[1]

According to Muslim belief, though inconsistent with historians, the founder of modern day Islam, Muhammad bin Abdullah, is a descendant of Ishmael. Muhammad lived during the sixth century AD and is referred to as "the Seal of the Prophets." His name means "highly praised." Although Muslims believe that there were other authentic prophets of Allah who came before him, Muhammad was the culmination of all the prophets—the final prophet—with none to follow him.

Two main sources exist from which we gain knowledge about the man named Muhammad bin Abdullah (the son of Abd Allah). One is a biography of Muhammad's life called the *Sira* (life). This account is believed to have been written about one 125 years after his death by Ibn Ishaq, a Muslim scholar. Around the ninth century AD and after some revision, it came to be regarded as the official account of Muhammad's life. The second source is the *Hadiths* (reports) which comprise a vast collection of individual reports concerning the words and deeds of Muhammad that were collected some two to three centuries after his death.

Muhammad was born approximately AD 570 into the leading tribe of Mecca, known as the Koreish. The character of Muhammad comes down by tradition. He is said to have been pure-hearted with a sweet and gentle disposition. As he grew older, his sense of honor, duty, and fidelity won him titles such as "the True," "the Upright One," and "the Trustworthy One." Because of his sensitivities, especially in light of the pagan culture of his time, he isolated himself from all the corruption.[2]

Muhammad was born to a base tribal environment at a time described by Muslims as "ignorant." People felt no obligation to anyone except their own tribe. This attitude, along with severe desert conditions and scarcity of material goods, made thievery and blood-thirsty barbarianism commonplace, including drunken orgies, gaming, and worse, the beastly spirits called *jinn* or demons—fantastic personifications of desert terrors. The conditions at the time and place that Muhammad entered history were replete with blood feuds, some that lasted for a half a century. The magistrate in the leading city of Mecca had collapsed and the influence of Islam had become ineffective. Clearly a deliverer was needed, which Muslims believe was Muhammad.

Muhammad often retreated to a cave at Mount Hira just outside the city of Mecca where he contemplated good and evil. He was driven not to accept the conditions of his times. Muhammad worshiped Allah—the Creator, Supreme Provider, and Determiner of Human Destiny. Muhammad was among the followers of Allah then called *hanifs*. Through vigils, some lasting all night, Muhammad sought Allah and became overwhelmed with the notion of Allah's greatness as the God, the One and Only, without rival.

Approximately AD 610, after many visits to the cave with increasing revelation, tradition states that Muhammad received his commission, similar to that which Muslims believe Abraham, Moses, Samuel, Isaiah, and Jesus experienced. This is referred to by Muslims as the Night of Power, when the Book was opened to a ready soul, and he became the Appointed One. Traditions state that he was visited by the angel Gabriel—the very same angel that announced the coming of Jesus to the Virgin Mary in Nazareth some six hundred years earlier. Supposedly, the angel's opening command to Muhammad was, "Proclaim!" Other versions state the angel commanded him, "Recite!" Gabriel made it known to Muhammad that he was to serve as the Messenger of God.

This was the first time that Muhammad believed that he received divine revelations in Arabic from Allah through Gabriel. These revelations would continue until his death and are cumulatively known as Qur'an, or Koran, meaning recitation. Muhammad reported these revelations verbatim to sympathetic family members and friends who either memorized them or wrote them down. To the Muslims the Koran is not a product of Muhammad's creative abilities, especially noting that tradition states he was illiterate. Rather, the Koran is considered the very words of God, which is the reason the Koran is considered sacred and highly revered by Muslims.

The Expansion of Islam

In time, Muhammad assembled a small band of devotees who rejected the pagan core of the traditional Meccan beliefs. Muhammad's followers were hated largely because of the complete disruption Muhammad's message brought to Mecca's governmental and religious way of life.

Muhammad's insistence that there is just one God, Allah, upset the long-held beliefs that Allah was the supreme God who governed the other 360 divinities. Moreover, Muhammad's claim that on Judgment Day Allah would overthrow anyone who mistreated the poor, and secure justice for all, was a condemnation against the blood-thirsty, cheating way of commerce that was common in Arabia. Muhammad's message and his followers were not merely rejected, they were vehemently opposed. Near the conclusion of a decade of his proclamations, Muhammad decided to make the trek north of Mecca to Medina. There his message was well received; he became recognized as Allah's messenger and his followers began to multiply.

Struggle for the minds of Arabia as a whole ensued and the Medinese quickly won a spectacular battle over a Meccan army that was many times larger. The Medinese interpreted their victory as a sign that angels in heaven were with them. Two years later, in AD 622, the Meccans regrouped and laid siege to Medina in a desperate attempt to force the Muslims to surrender unconditionally. This attempt failed and Muhammad's role among the people was sealed as both prophet and political leader.

Muhammad's acceptance in Medina marks the real beginning of Islam. At this point, Muhammad was able to establish a community centered on belief that Allah was the one true God and he, Muhammad, was the Messenger of Allah. The people elevated him further to the role of civil ruler, establishing the *umma* (Muslim state), which is a very important concept for Muslims. The founding of this first Muslim state was so important that the Muslim calendar was changed to mark AD 622 as the beginning of the Muslim calendar.[3]

Tradition states that after this, Muhammad made his way to the famous Ka'ba (again, believed to have been built by Abraham), and he rededicated it to Allah.[4] By AD 628, after many more bloody sieges conducted by Muhammad against Meccan trade convoys or caravans, Mecca was forced to sign a truce-treaty with Muhammad. This made it possible for Muslims to make the pilgrimages down to Mecca to pay homage to the prophet at his birthplace.

When Muhammad died, in AD 632, he had virtually all of Arabia under his control, both religiously and politically, through various battles and sieges that were won aggressively. At the height of the Arab conquests, the empire of the Arab people extended from the shores of the Atlantic Ocean to the confines of China. These world conquerors possessed an empire greater than that of Rome at its zenith. In their period of unprecedented expansion of the Arab empire, Islam rose to greatness.[5]

Before the century closed, his followers had conquered Armenia, Persia, Syria, Palestine, Iraq, North Africa, and Spain and had crossed the Pyrenees into France. Were it not for their defeat by Charles Martel (grandfather of Charlemagne the Great) in the Battle of Tours in AD 733, the entire Western world might today be Muslim.[6]

Distinctions within Islam

There are major parties or sects within Islam today. To understand these we need to understand the progression of leadership that occurred after Muhammad's death. Because Muhammad did not explicitly appoint anyone to take his place, close supporters of Muhammad when he was alive were the next leaders of Islam. The first three historical leaders of Islam are referred to as *caliphs.*

Caliph Abu Bakr led the faith for three years from AD 632 to AD 634. He was followed by Caliph Umar from AD 634 to AD 644. Shortly before his death, Umar appointed a group of men to elect the next caliph. The group selected Uthman, a prominent man of Mecca. In these years following Mohammad's death, things went fairly well. Beginning AD 656, the fourth caliph chosen was Ali, who was also Muhammad's son-in-law and married to the prophet's daughter Fatima. During his five-year rule, there was unrest among the people. A great divide rose up among the faithful. Some were loyal to Caliph Abu Bakr and Caliph Uthman, while others were loyal to the leadership of Caliph Ali. Tension grew, creating two fiercely opposing groups—those in favor of the family line leadership and those opposed. A rebellion against caliph Ali resulted bringing several years of Muslim civil wars. Ultimately Mawiyah, a relative of Caliph Uthman, emerged from the strife. He ruled Islam in a manner far more akin to a monarchy. Upon his death his son, Yazid, succeeded him as the sixth caliph.

This outraged those who believed the rulership should have remained according to Muhammad's bloodline. In retaliation, these sought the help of the son of Caliph Ali, named Hussein, and instigated a rebellion. The rebellion was bloody and ended with Hussein viciously slain at the battle of Karbala in central Iraq in the year AD 680. From these two positions, one believing that leadership should remain in the bloodline of Muhammad and those who supported the appointment of Yazid, we have the *Shi'ite* and the *Sunni* traditions within Islam.

Sunnis support the appointment of Yazid and are referred to as the traditionalists. They comprise about 85 percent of the Muslim population. This group accepted the consensus of those who appointed the caliphs who today continue in this tradition through a council of scholars. This is a group of men highly trained in the law (*Sharia*) of Islam. Sunnis do not accept the veneration of mere men to Islamic saints. Further, they believe that each person is responsible for his/her salvation.

Shi'ites uphold the memory of Muhammad with a deep passion and represent about 15 percent of the Muslim population—a minority, although they represent the majority in places such as Iraq and Iran. Successors to Yazid at some point were no longer referred to as caliphs, but as *Imam*, which means leader. Imams were considered to be men with special closeness to Allah who could intercede for the destiny of the followers. Therefore, they could become the objects of religious devotion. This group believes that *the twelfth Imam,* who lived and disappeared in the ninth century, will reappear at the end of history to restore justice and establish Shi'ite Islam in the world. Martyrdom is highly esteemed by this group, as seen by the brutal slaying of Hussein, son of Caliph Ali.

Islam continued to grow in the region of Arabia, spreading even to Palestine, Morocco, and Spain. The Islamic elite were more and more criticized for their worldliness, as expressed in their wielding of power and possessions. In response to this, a mass movement known as *Sufism* emerged. Sufism is identified as the mystical branch of Islam. Sufis tended to bypass the hierarchy of Islam, believing people could create their own contact with Allah. This was utterly unacceptable to the traditional scholars who worked to preserve the teachings of Muhammad as written in the Koran.[7]

The Koran

It is important to understand Islam considers the Koran as the source of all truth, believing that it is "God-made text." The Koran to the Muslim is far more than just a book—it is a literal extension of God. Although this is a highly contentious subject, the Koran itself most likely also suffered during this time of establishing Muhammad's successors. As stated before, Muhammad claimed that he received the contents of the Koran from Angel Gabriel with the command to recite what he heard. Muslims believe the messages began in AD 610 and continued until Muhammad's death in AD 632. Muhammad would recite verses of the Koran to his followers and instruct them to memorize it.

Muslim and non-Muslim scholars disagree on whether Muhammad penned any of the messages or if this task began with the first caliph, Abu Bakr (AD 632–634), Caliph Umar (AD 634–644). or potentially Caliph Uthman (AD 653–656).

Most Sunni and Shi'ite scholars believe that the Koran was compiled in its entirety at the time of the prophet's death, though not necessarily written down. Many believe that the *surahs* (chapters) of the Koran were collated by Abu Bakr and that his successor, Caliph Umar, brought them together into a single volume. Unknown numbers of copies were made from these two collections. Then under the next leader, Caliphate of Uthman, all copies of the Koran were ordered to be brought in, and any that deviated from his version were burned. Muslims who had memorized the entire Koran from the versions Caliph Uthman were vehemently opposed. Shi'ite Muslims claim that Caliph Uthman intentionally eliminated many passages from the

Koran which related to Ali and the succession of leadership which was to occur after Muhammad's death.

A post in the *Islam Forum* online reads, "Modern Muslims assert that the current Koran is identical to that recited by Muhammad. But earlier Muslim researchers were more flexible. 'Uthman, A'isha, and Ibn Ka'b (among others) all insisted that much of the Koran had been lost. Codices were made by different scholars (e.g. Ibn Mas'ud, Ubai ibn Ka'b, 'Ali, Abu Bakr, al-Aswad). 'Uthman's codex supposedly standardized the consonantal text [where no vowels are written], yet consonantal variations persisted into the fourth century. An unpointed and unvowelled script contributed to the problem. Also, although 'Uthman tried to destroy rival codices, variant readings survived. Standardization was not actually achieved until the tenth century under the influence of Ibn Mujahid. Even he admitted fourteen versions of the Koran [existed]. These are not merely differences in recitation; they are actual written variations."[8]

Because of the Muslims sacred reverence for the Koran and their belief about who should be Muhammad's successors, there is a notable lack of critical scholarship on the Koran. The critical scholarship that does exist is highly contentious and difficult to confirm.

The Teachings of Islam

There are six basic doctrines every Muslim is required to believe:

1. There is one true God and His name is Allah.
2. The chief angel is Gabriel, who was instrumental in revealing the visions to Muhammad. *Jinn* (genies or demons) exist too and the chief of the *jinn* is Shaytan (Satan).
3. There are four books Muslims consider inspired: the Torah of Moses (first five books of the Old Testament), the

91

Zabur (Psalms of David), the Injil (the gospel of Jesus as a Prophet only), and the Koran. Muslims believe the first three contain errors because they have been altered by Jews and Christians. Since they believe that the Koran is God's most recent and final word, it is viewed as superior to all other writings.

4. There will be a final Judgment Day when the dead will be resurrected. Allah will judge each individual according to his/her deeds and send them to heaven or hell. Heaven, according to Islam, is a place of sensual pleasure.

5. The prophets are limited to twenty-eight in the Koran. The most well-known include Adam, Noah, Abraham, Moses, David, Jonah, and Jesus. Muhammad is the last and greatest prophet.

6. Predestination for each individual has been predetermined by Allah according to His pleasure and no one can change what He has decreed.[9]

There are five basic practices of the Muslim faith: Confession or Declaration of Faith in Allah (*Shahada*), Prayer (*Salat*), Almsgiving or Charity (*Zakat*), Fasting (*Sawm* or *Ramadan*), and Pilgrimage (*Hajj*). These are referred to as the *Five Pillars of the Islamic Faith*. Struggle to propagate the faith of Islam around the world is known as *Jihad*. Some include Jihad and claim there are *Six Pillars of the Islamic Faith,* while others refer to only Five Pillars, leaving Jihad separate.[10]

Muslims do not believe that Jesus was anything more than a prophet—Allah's messenger. They do not believe He was crucified on the cross. They believe that Allah spared Jesus from such a disgraceful death and took Him up to Himself.[11]

The Islamic View of Humanity and Destiny

The Koran teaches that *Iblis* or *Shaytan* (Satan), which means "banished," refused to be subordinate to the first created human being, Adam, as Allah instructed. Satan's pride and arrogance caused him to disobey Allah. In response, according to the Koran, Allah stated, "I am placing a representative (a temporary god) on Earth. They [the beings Allah was addressing] said, 'Will You place therein one who will spread evil therein and shed blood, while we sing Your praises, glorify You, and uphold Your absolute authority?'" (al-Baqarah 2:30). Muslims believe that Satan was banished to the earth with the task of leading astray, through corruption, those who do not worship Allah.

Islam teaches that man has the faculty of being able to distinguish and choose between good and evil. It's believed that "Allah has gifted man with the ability to distinguish between good and evil, so Allah inspired the human soul its corruption and it righteousness. Allah made man possess the ability to choose freely between these two ways, and clarified to him that his goal in this life is to raise himself well and elevate himself toward virtue." Unlike Christianity, Islam does not teach that mankind is born with a sin nature; instead people choose to sin. Therefore, there is no need for salvation. Instead man merely needs to sincerely worship Allah and resist the corruption of Satan. Muslims believe that man is responsible and accountable and he will get the results of his deeds.[12]

Muslims believe in Judgment Day or the Day of Judgment. According to Islam, human beings have eternal souls destined for either *Janna* (paradise/heaven) or *Jahannam* (hell/pit of blazing fire). In the Koran, the physical characteristics of paradise are described in great detail. Muslims believe some people will go directly to paradise while some will spend a period in hell for the time necessary to atone for some of their sins, while others will live in hell forever. There is no assurance of entering Janna and neither is there requirement to keep the laws perfectly. It is unclear where the cut off line is for Allah's basis of granting entrance to Janna.

Some believe that each person must pay for his/her own sins. Other Muslims think simply believing in Allah and doing good deeds means paradise awaits them. For yet another group, entrance to paradise is solely on the basis of Allah's mercy.

The topic of Jihad is important to understand. We, in western culture, have heard this word and many do not understand its meaning. Jihad is a word that for most Muslims literally means "struggle" or "striving" as in the struggle to be a good Muslim. Since there are many struggles in life, there are several kinds of Jihad recognized within Islam: "Jihad of the heart" is the struggle against oneself; "Jihad of the tongue" or "Jihad of the pen" involves persuasion, exhortation, and instruction for the cause of Islam; "Jihad of the sword" is armed fighting or holy war and so on. Still, the primary meaning of Jihad is physical combat. According to Reuven Firestone, professor of medieval Judaism and Islam at Hebrew Union College in Los Angeles, "When the term is used without qualifiers such as 'of the heart' or 'of the tongue' it is universally understood as war on behalf of Islam (equivalent to 'Jihad of the sword'), and the merits of engaging in such Jihad are described plentifully in the most respected religious works."[13]

There are some texts of the Koran that refer to Jihad as military struggle. Sura 2:190–193 is one example. This text encourages Muslims to fight, for the sake of Allah, those that fight against you, claiming that idolatry is more grievous than bloodshed. However, it instructs not to attack unbelievers first—respond only if they attack first. Many of today's Muslims stress that the Islamic terrorism suffered around the world is in contradiction to the Koran's teaching. Others believe it is wholly consistent with the Koran's instruction.

Jihad includes a religious war against unbelievers with the object of converting them to Islam or subduing all opposition (see Koran 9:5; 4:76; 2:214; 8:39). It is the sacred duty of the Muslim nation to ensure that Islam triumphs over all religions. The general duty of the nation as a whole, not of individuals, is to ensure this triumph.

Modern Islam

In his early years, Muhammad spread Islam by teaching and persuasion. Several early Meccan *suras* stated that he was sent only to preach. A change occurred when at Medina, Muhammad declared that God had allowed him and his followers to defend themselves against infidels. Later he proclaimed that he had divine leave to attack them and set up the true faith by the sword. Muhammad himself fought in nine battles and ordered many more.[14]

Contemporary Islami holds that Islam is now under attack and, therefore, experts explain, Jihad is now a war of defense. As such, it has become not only a collective duty, but an individual duty without restrictions or limitations. To the Islamists, Jihad is a total, all-encompassing duty to be carried out by all Muslims—men and women, young and old. All infidels, without exception, are to be fought and annihilated and no weapons or types of warfare are barred. Furthermore, according to contemporary Islamists, current Muslim rulers allied with the West are considered apostates and infidels. One major ideological influence in Islamist thought was Sayyid Qutb. Qutb, an Egyptian, was the leader of the Muslim Brotherhood movement. He was convicted of treason for plotting to assassinate Egyptian president Gamal Abd Al-Nasser and was executed in 1966. He wrote extensively on a wide range of Islamic issues. According to Qutb, "There are two parties in all the world: the Party of Allah and the Party of Satan–the Party of Allah, which stands under the banner of Allah and bears His insignia, and the Party of Satan, which includes every community, group, race, and individual that does not stand under the banner of Allah."[15]

Christianity is the subject of the next chapter.

Chapter Ten

Faith Findings—Christianity

In this postmodern culture, people are not only adding to their religious beliefs tenets from other opposing religions and philosophies; they are also reinterpreting classic or orthodox Christian beliefs. If you've never understood the basic orthodox Christian beliefs, this chapter should be helpful.

Christianity's Origin

Some say that Christianity was founded initially as the small religious movement among some Jews when the prophet and teacher named Jesus, who was crucified by the Roman government, became the focal point. In a sense this is true. but it is not complete. It's more accurate to say that New Testament Christianity is a continuation of Old Testament Judaism.

Like Judaism and Islam, Christianity claims that Abraham is the first God-appointed patriarch for their religious beliefs. However, Christians identify the origin, their faith—that is, the offer of a restored relationship with God—to God's promise that He would send a Deliverer or Redeemer expressed in Genesis 3. Strongly identifying with Judaism, but interpreting scriptures differently, Christianity has its roots in Judaism.

As previously written, Christians and Jews share the same sacred scriptures. The Christian's Old Testament contains the very same books as the Jewish scriptures, just in a different order.

The whole of the Christian Bible contains the *Old Testament* writings penned before the birth of Jesus, as well as the *New Testament* writings penned after the birth, life, death and resurrection of Jesus, known as "the Christ." The word "Christ" is an English adaptation of the Greek word *Christos,* which is used to translate the Jewish word *Messiah.* Christ, *Christos,* and *Messiah* literally mean "anointed." The Anointed One is the title early believers gave to Jesus, recognizing Him as the expected Deliverer, Redeemer, or Savior—all being terms that are used interchangeably by Christians.

Christians view Jesus as the promised Deliverer or Redeemer. Genesis 3:14–15 reveals God's promise to provide a Deliverer who will ultimately secure relief from the pain, suffering, and evil of this world and restoration of personal relationship with God for those who believe—for those who have faith in God's promise in the same manner as Abraham. Christianity, then, is the New Testament continuation of the Old Testament promise.

There are some theologians who state categorically that there is no salvation or redemption for anyone who has not personally come to believe in and receive Jesus as their Savior. However, there is another view supported by the Old and New Testament scriptures. It is generally accepted among Christians that God will hold people accountable for their response to the revelation of truth God has individually provided them. God reveals truth in many ways—through creation (Romans 1:18–25), through moral conscious (Romans 2:12–16), through knowledge of the person of Jesus Christ, and other ways. Dan Story explains in his book *Defending Your Faith* how those who have never heard the gospel message will be judged according to the information about God they do have (First Timothy 1:13; Romans 2:13–16; 5:15; Acts 17:30): "God will judge according to what we know, not according to what we do not know. This implies, of course, that those of us who have heard the gospel message and reject it are far more deserving of punishment than those who have never heard of Jesus at all (Luke 12:47–48; Matthew 10:11–15; John 9:41)."

The Christian Bible

The manuscript evidence in support of the Bible is unique in comparison to the documents of religious authority for all other religions (discussed in chapter twelve). Christians believe that the entire Bible is without conflict or error. Neither does it have any substantive changes when compared to its earliest known manuscripts. The Bible's oldest known manuscripts are older by at least one thousand years, in comparison to the available texts of all other religions sacred writings—except, of course, Judaism. Therefore, Christians claim it to be an easy application of faith to believe the Bible has remained unchanged since it was originally penned. The critical conclusion of Christians is that the Bible is divinely inspired.[1]

The Christian version of the Old Testament text is arranged in thirty-six books, in contrast to twenty-four books in the Jewish scriptures. The traditional view about the origin of the Old Testament writings is that Moses and Joshua were inspired by God to record the events of creation and the Creation of mankind as revealed to them by God, along with the history of humanity. This created the first five books. Subsequent books were penned by various men also believed to be inspired by God. New Testament scriptures provide eyewitness testimonies about the life, death, and resurrection of Jesus, about His teachings, and about the early church and other revelations given to men by God to be written down.

99

The sixty-six books for both the Old and New Testaments were penned by forty different authors over a span of approximately fifteen hundred years in three different languages—Hebrew, Aramaic, and Greek, covering hundreds of subjects. Yet amazingly, with such a vast compilation and without any personal collaboration, there is no conflict of information. From the Old Testament through the New Testament, there is one constant theme—God's redemption of mankind.

The Bible is considered by Christians to be the revealed Word of God. There are additional books Catholics use that Protestants do not—Tobit, Judith, Wisdom of Solomon, Ecclesiasticus (Sirach), Baruch (including the Letters of Jeremiah), I and II Maccabees, and additions to Daniel and Esther. These books were included in the *Septuagint*, a Greek translation of the Hebrew Old Testament. Early church fathers relied on the Septuagint because they could not read Hebrew and sometimes quoted these books as scripture. The status of these books continued to be debated throughout the Middle Ages.

At the time of the Protestant Reformation (sixteenth century AD), leaders of the movement decided that because the additional books covering the pre–New Testament era were not in the Hebrew scriptures, they should not be in the Protestant Bible (though they were included in early editions of the King James). Catholics, at the Council of Trent (AD 1546), decided to continue teaching the "deutero-canonical" books. This is why there are differences in the New Testament used by Protestants and Catholics.[2]

The Christian View of God, Creation and the Origin of Evil

As do Jews, Christians accept the historical account of the origin of all that exists as described in Genesis—the universe, the earth, all life, and the dual existence of both good and evil. Christians believe that evil was ushered into this world by the choice Adam and Eve made to disobey God. Up until that point, all of creation was good and utterly void of corruption. The choice to disobey or rebel is referred to as *sin*. Christians understand that sin is not only viewed as the act of rejecting or rebelling against God and His instructions; it is also the consequential condition imposed upon all humanity as a result of the original rebellion.

Christianity is a monotheistic faith that believes there is only one God. But, unique to the Christian interpretation of God described in the Old Testament is the concept of *the Trinity*. Christians believe that God is triune in nature—or "three persons in one." He is *God the Father,* or Creator; *God the Son,* or Redeemer/Deliverer; and *God the Holy Spirit,* or Power. The Christian God is also referred to as the Holy Trinity.

Genesis states that mankind was created in God's image. Christians understand that this refers to attributes such as knowledge, righteousness and holiness, logic, morality, independent will, distinct personality, and eternal spirit.[3] Genesis also states that God gave humanity authority over all creation. Most Christian denominations agree with what has been written so far to describe the Christian faith. Yet, as with all religions, there are various sects or denominations that disagree on doctrine interpretation.

Continuing with the traditional understanding of the Christian faith, the book of Genesis reveals that God created Adam in a perfect and lush environment called the Garden of Eden. God instructed Adam that he could eat of any tree in the garden except the Tree of Knowledge of Good and Evil. God made it clear to Adam that if he ate of this particular tree he would die. This referred to spiritual death, where the holy spiritual condition of Adam would become corrupt—his very nature would be altered. The word *holy* literally means "to be set apart." The implied meaning is to be set apart from all that is not good and pure.

In this garden, Adam was given the task of naming all the animals as they were brought before him by God. Adam saw that all the animals were created in pairs, male and female, and realized there was no female like him. God declared that it was not good for man to be alone. Clearly God was not finished with creation. He next caused Adam to fall into a deep sleep and took bone and flesh from Adam's side to create Eve. Adam's mental, emotional, spiritual connection with Eve provided him his physical counterpart. Adam and Eve's physical connection, with all its God-given pleasures, provided the means for them to procreate.

With every God-created reality, there is spiritual significance. The sacred union between man and woman as ordained by God is an earthly depiction of the intimate relationship God intended humans to have with Him—in all holiness, spirit to spirit. This is the kind of relationship Adam and Eve originally had with God. God intended for Adam and Eve, as the beginning of all humanity, to multiply. Additionally, God intended humanity to care for and have dominion over all creation with His guidance. Both Adam and Eve enjoyed God's presence through spiritual communion with Him as they lived in the Garden of Eden.

From the book of Genesis, Christians account the entrance of evil—pain, suffering, sickness, and death upon all creation—to the influence of *Satan*. Satan, the enemy of God, deceived Eve about God's motive for restricting them from eating from the fruit of the Tree of Knowledge of Good and Evil. Satan boldly told the woman that she would not die if she ate of that tree, contrary to God's clear pronouncement. Satan declared, "God knows that in the day you eat of it your eyes will be opened, and you will be like God, knowing good and evil."[4]

With doubt planted in her mind and the appeal that she could be like God, Eve took the fruit and ate it. Adam, who was with her, quite apparently did not do enough to stop Eve, and he witnessed the transformation of her soul and spirit. He was now in a place to choose to obey God and remain in communion with Him, or to disobey and join his wife—the one who was created from his own flesh and bone. Adam was in a very difficult place. He chose to eat of the forbidden fruit, and the moment he did, his soul and spirit also died, bringing corruption to mankind. Instead of listening only to God and obeying Him, Adam listened to his wife and did as she suggested. Although both Adam and Eve disobeyed, God holds Adam primarily responsible. R. C. Sproul, a well-known Christian theologian, professor, author, and pastor, explains in his article "Adam's Fall and Mine": "Adam was the first human being created. He stands at the head of the human race. He was placed in the garden to act not only for himself but for all of his future descendants." The New Testament supports this in Romans 5:12–19, where we read that it was through one man's sin that all of creation suffers.

Recognizing Satan as ultimately responsible, God cursed him. God promised to put enmity between Satan and the woman and between Satan's seed (offspring) and the woman's seed. In this promise from Genesis 3:14–15, God promises to ultimately provide a Deliverer—a way for human redemption.[5]

God declared to the woman that now her sorrow and conception would be multiplied, and in pain, she would bring forth children, and He explained that she will be ruled by her husband.[6] Sin separated Eve from being ruled by God. Because Adam heeded the voice of his wife rather than God's, God declared that the ground from which he came would be cursed and produce thistles and thorns. From that day forward, man would work hard to produce his food until the day he dies and returns to the dust from which he came.[7]

Because Adam and Eve sinned and acted according to their own free will, in disobedience to God, their very nature was altered, just as God forewarned. Consequently, every human being born ever since has inherited the same spiritually dead condition. The promise of God to provide a Deliverer, however, is humanity's hope.

The Expansion of Christianity

Christians, Jews, and Muslims each lay claim to Abraham as the patriarchal father first mentioned in Genesis 11. God made an everlasting covenant or promise to Abraham that through his seed (offspring) he would be the father of many nations.

From Genesis 12–21 much of the life of Abram (later named Abraham) is recorded. From the seed of Eve to the lineage of Abraham, God planned the heritage of the promised Redeemer. God promised Abram that he would bear a son and Abram would become the father of many nations. Abram believed God for the fulfillment of God's promise, and lived expectantly.

However, since after many years of Abram's wife Sarai (later named Sarah) was still barren, she recommended her husband to take her Egyptian maidservant, Hagar. This being acceptable according to the customs of the day, Sarai hoped that through Hagar she may have a child. But Hagar conceived, which became a matter of contention between the two women. In effort to escape Sarai's harsh treatment, Hagar fled from her presence. An Angel of the Lord appeared to Hagar and spoke to her in her distress. He instructed her to return to her mistress and submit herself. Through this angel, God promised to multiply her descendants exceedingly. He revealed that she bore a son who was to be named Ishmael. God stated that he would grow to be a wild man with his hand against every man and every man's hand against him.

Ishmael was born because of Abram and Sarai's action, but he was not the son of promise. God intended the offspring of Abram and Sarai to fulfill His plan.

Several years later God appeared to Abram. God again declared that Abram would be the father of many nations and kings and that he would inherit the land of Canaan as an everlasting possession and that He would be their God. God pronounced that Abram would conceive with his wife Sarai. Abram laughed at the prospect, considering that he was ninety-nine and Sarai ninety—well past childbearing years. Abram pleaded with God that Ishmael could inherit the promise. But, God affirmed His Word, and required that when the son is born, he be named Isaac—it was through Isaac that God intended to fulfill the original promise of a Deliverer. At this time God changed their names to Abraham and Sarah. Abraham then honored the covenant by way of circumcision as God had instructed.

At the specific time appointed by God Abraham and Sarah conceived a boy whom they named Isaac. When he was eight days old, Isaac was circumcised in keeping with God's commandment as a sign of the covenant. Abraham was one hundred years old when Isaac was born.

In time, Hagar and Ishmael were sent away. God assured Abraham that he should not be displeased because He would also make a nation through his son Ishmael. Ishmael's blessing was to be fruitful with exceedingly many offspring, that he would bear twelve princes and be made a great nation. With this, Ishmael departed from the family of Abraham with his mother and took a wife from the land of Egypt. It is from Ishmael that many of the people groups we know as Arabs descended. Isaac, however, was the son of promise who would carry forth the covenant God had made with Abraham, according to the Christian beliefs.[8]

The descendants of Abraham are listed in the Old and New Testaments. From Adam to Abraham to Isaac to Jacob (whose name was changed to Israel), through King David and beyond, Christians trace the lineage of the promised Deliverer/Redeemer from Adam directly up to Jesus.[9]

The Christian View of Jesus

Christians believe that Jesus was and is the promised Redeemer who was born of a virgin named Mary in approximately 4 BC. Because God had promised to send a Deliverer/Redeemer, Christians refer to the person of Jesus as "God's word (promise) made flesh."

According to the Bible, God "overshadowed" Mary and miraculously united the human egg with the divine counterpart, allowing Jesus to be conceived. This made him both fully human and fully God. The New Testament reveals that Jesus willingly laid down His divinity and lived completely in His humanity while on earth. Although He was tempted to sin in every way common to man, He was the only human to never sin. This leads up to the very reason for His existence. As the only sinless Man He was the only sacrifice able to satisfy the debt of sins for the whole world. According to the Bible, Christians believe that by faith in the life, death, and resurrection of Jesus on the first Easter morning as the Deliverer/Redeemer, anyone who desires can be saved from sin. Through faith in Jesus, a person is restored to a spiritually alive condition and enjoys personal relationship with God. Christians are those who have placed their faith in Jesus, as their personal Savior from sin, whose sacrifice allows them to face a final Judgment Day without personal condemnation. Jesus paid the debt of sin once and for all who wills to believe and receive Him by faith.

Hebrews 9:22 states, "Without the shedding of blood, there is no remission of sin." So it was the sacrifice of Jesus that links the Old

Testament sacrifices with the New Testament sacrifice, Jesus. Genesis reveals that once Adam and Eve confessed their disobedience, God covered their bodies with animal skin. Hence, the first animal sacrifice demanded the shedding of blood to *cover* the sin, until the time of the promised Redeemer whose sacrifice would *cleanse* believers from sin. The Old Testament animal sacrifice system was established by God to provide a covering for sin, for all who obeyed and believed in God and His promises. Christians believe that this system also provided a "type" for the ultimate sacrifice—Jesus, the promised Deliverer. They believe that all who by faith believe God for His promised Redeemer are saved. Old Testament believers look forward to the fulfillment of God's promise while New Testament believers look back to the promise fulfilled in the life, death, and resurrection of Jesus.

Those who believe and receive Jesus as their personal Savior by faith are given a new spirit, referred to as being "born again," and they receive the indwelling of the Holy Spirit to transform and guide them.[10]

The Bible and other historical documents reveal that Jesus was born approximately 4 BC and was crucified at age thirty in approximately AD 33. Beyond the New Testament's recorded witness of Jesus' crucifixion and resurrection, there are additional ancient historical documents that provide considerable evidence about Jesus.

The Teachings of Christianity

As with all religious faiths, there are many sects or denominations within Christianity. However, the five specific basic beliefs of the faith, referred to as "the Essentials of Christianity," are as follows:

1. Belief that salvation is attained by faith in Jesus Christ alone.

2. Belief that Jesus Christ was God incarnate, both fully God and fully human, who died for our sins as the only suitable substitute and sacrifice.

3. Belief that Jesus was bodily resurrected from the dead and now lives to ever intercede for those who believe.

4. Belief that God is a unique Deity, triune in nature: God the Father, God the Son, and God the Holy Spirit, who is the Creator of all that exists, and Supreme over all.

5. Belief that the Bible, both the Old and New Testaments, is the inspired and infallible written Word of God.

According to the Christian faith, if a person believes in his/her mind and confesses from his/her heart these five basic tenets, they are transformed from one whose spirit is dead and headed for hell to one that is made alive, or *born again* by the Holy Spirit, and destined for heaven.

There are additional points beyond these five essentials for salvation that Christians also agree on. The most significant of these points is that Jesus will return again to claim all who belong to Him and to judge all who do not—beginning with the dead first then those who are living. The Christian faith holds that every person will be judged. But, those whose faith is in Jesus will be completely pardoned of their sin and granted entry into heaven, where all the faithful will dwell in communion with God.

Christians believe, according to John 3:18, that anyone who does not choose God through faith in Jesus Christ is choosing to be forever separated from Him and all that is good. The Christians position is that God does not send people to hell—people make that choice for themselves by denying Jesus.

The Christian Bible describes heaven as a place where there is no weeping or sorrow, only joy; there is no marrying of men and women, no Jew, no Gentile, no slave, no free; rather, all will be as one, devoted to Jesus. Hell is described as a place of fire—and eternal torment, a place intended by God for Satan and his followers—not originally intended for mankind.

Because of the revealed character of God in the Old and New Testaments, through creation and through His historical intervention with mankind, Christians ascribe only good and loving attributes to God. The Bible reveals that God's love for His creation is pure, set apart as holy and unique. By His love, He is motivated to continually work to redeem His creation through His offer of *salvation* (redemption from sin) through faith in Jesus Christ. Salvation is a three-part transformation that includes *justification* (saved from the penalty of sin), *sanctification* (saved from the power of sin), and *glorification* (saved from the presence of sin).

Salvation is God's personal deliverance of His people from the ravages of sin in this world. "God's people," (more fully understood in the New Testament era), is anyone who chooses to place their faith in Him, as the Father Creator, Son the Savior, and Holy Spirit the Power. Unlike all other religious beliefs, Christianity offers transformation and a hope with a heavenly future *by faith alone.* All other religious beliefs require specific "works" to satisfy or appease their God or process. First John 4:8 in the New Testament describes God with this statement: "God is love."

Distinctions within Christianity

Within Christianity, there has been a significant movement away from long-held beliefs, such as taking the Bible literally, the existence of hell, life after death, the existence of heaven, the need for salvation, belief in a literal being known as Satan, the definition of marriage, creation by God's intelligent design, and more. Some denominations have strayed so far from doctrines central to Christianity that they actually hold beliefs that oppose the scriptures. Thus they are not at all Christian, though they continue to identify themselves as Christian. Other denominations have altered or added to the meaning of the scriptures resulting in significant differences among those who profess to be Christians.

Part Three

Deciding Truth

Chapter Eleven

Faith Reconsidered

My effort up to this point has been to properly identify truth and reveal the unique distinctions of the various religious faiths. By learning a specific religion's distinctions we can see that they cannot be combined or harmonized in any manner. People who attempt to combine the tenets of various religious faiths are choosing a belief system that is utterly unstable. Referring back to the exploration about truth itself in chapter three, we've determined that only one thing can be true and all opposing matters are false. So, at this juncture, my goal is to help you reconsider what you believe in order to be certain your faith is based on truth.

In my personal quest to find truth, I concluded that Christianity not only made the most logical sense; it also appealed greatly to my soul in a way that transcends rational thought. As I wrote about in chapter one, although I'd been introduced to Christianity as a young girl, I wasn't committed to the faith. It was my personal crisis that caused me to explore the various faiths in order to intentionally examine what I believed and why I believed it. Through this process, I arrived at a confident faith in Christ. After I learned about the origins, history, beliefs, and impact other religions have had on the world, Christianity became the most compelling for me. It's the only religious belief that offers solutions to the problems of life and provides a confident hope. Christianity presents God, who Himself paid the debt owed by humanity so that He would not lose those who want to be in relationship with Him. This is very different from all other religious beliefs that require man to do something to find peace. The mercy and long-suffering of God are more evidence of His love for each of us. What you believe is a conclusion for you to make. It is my prayer that as you continue reading this book, you will arrive at a faith conviction that you are truly confident in too.

Conflict with Religion

With the previous chapters, I attempted to describe each of the top five major world religious faiths and the secular points of view. I've presented the origins and the basic premise of the different religious beliefs. It's important to again note that within each of the religious faiths there are sects or denominations that include additional or different doctrines. Expressions of the faith differ within each religion according to denomination, sect, or faction, from moderate to extreme.

History is replete with religious wars which are caused and/or justified by religious differences. In fact, many distinctions within a particular religious faith and/or entirely new factions have been born of conflict. An excellent visual resource to see the expansion of the five major religions over at least five thousand years can be viewed online at mapsofwar.com, http://www.mapsofwar.com/ind/history-of-religion.html.

Clearly no religion is without responsibility for causing devastating conflict in the world, but rather than make a sweeping generalization, wouldn't it be more accurate to say that no religion is without denominations or sects that operate in the extreme? I firmly conclude the latter. Our goal here is to discover and live our lives on the basis of truth—the whole truth. This means we must work at having an honest and balanced perspective and do our best to simply weigh the evidence.

The Intention of Religion

To many people, the term *religious war* is a contradiction in and of itself. This is especially true when considering the purpose or intention of religion. According to *The Word Book Dictionary*, the word *religion* comes from the Latin word *religio*, which has a meaning influenced by the verb *religare*, to bind, in the sense of to "place an obligation on." *The World Book Dictionary* defines *obligation* as "duty," which in turn is defined as "a thing which a person ought to do; a thing which is right to do." The words *ought* and *duty* with reference to "the right thing to do" implies human obligation to a universal moral code. Again, no one ever raises their hand when asked, "Who in this room wants to base their life on a lie?" This single question reveals that we innately understand the difference between a lie and truth. It also reveals that humans universally consider a lie undesirable, or "bad," and the truth is considered desirable, or "good." Morality then must be recognized as a code that is intrinsic to humanity. With the exception of those who are sadly deranged, we commonly agree that murder, stealing, cheating, and lying are "bad."

If there is a moral law (which I believe has been sufficiently established to exist), it logically follows that there must be a moral Law-Giver—an authority who established the laws of morality. Simply considering the Latin origin of the word religion, it seems that "obligation" or "duty" is due to the moral Law-Giver—even though many people are not willing to acknowledge one such Supreme Being.

Much about religion stems from man-made ideals, institutions, regulations, and rituals. Religions of all types both unite and divide people. All religions seek to discover the solution to pain, suffering, and evil. The religions considered in this book represent ideas, philosophies, and efforts to make sense of this world. Most of these religions seek to discover our ultimate escape, our ultimate destination and our reason for being. Each is very distinct in regard to defining the existence and character of "God" and His, or Its intention toward man.

Seeking Truth in Religion

Rather than a embarking on a quest to find the right religion, consider the merit of seeking truth. If we are confident that we have placed our faith in truth, then our faith conviction is certain. With sufficient objective, verifiable evidence for what can be proven, we can believe what is yet to be proven. This is to have a confident faith. Seeking truth in order to have a confident faith requires that we examine the specific truth claims of the various religions.

Naturally, our own cultural experiences will cause us to be attracted to certain beliefs. Houston Smith, in his book *The World's Religions: Our Great Wisdom Traditions*, wrote, "Every religion mixes universal principles with local peculiarities. The former, when lifted out and made clear, speak to what is generically human in us all. The latter, rich compounds of rites and legends are not easy for outsiders to comprehend."[1] Because of this, I sought the input of individuals who were reared in each of the five main religions. Each individual came to a point in his/her life when he/she questioned why he/she believed as he/she did. As a result of their own quest for truth, their contribution to this book is invaluable.

Anyone who honestly evaluates their religious beliefs will ask certain questions. I think the following will be most frequently asked, though you may have more of your own to add:

- Which religious faith seems to best answer man's common and most probing questions?
- Which religious faith has historically produced the greatest good?
- Which religious faith makes the most sense?
- Which religious faith offers real and certain hope?
- Which religious faith best promotes love and compassion for humanity?
- Which religious faith genuinely appeals to my spirit?
- Which religious faith has the most objective verifiable evidence allowing me to believe for what is yet to be proven?

No one consciously chooses to live his/her life on the basis of a lie, but we cannot know if what we believe is true without careful examination.

The following are true-life stories of individuals who bravely examined what they believed. Like me, they all came to a point in his or her life that caused them to question what they believed. They share their journey of discovery and their personal conclusion. These stories are printed here just as they wrote them.

Judaism: Finding the Messiah

Aaron and Diane Schneiderman from Southern California share their story of realizing Yeshua (the Hebrew name for Jesus) is the Messiah.

Many years ago, when the only religion I (Aaron) had was the fact that I knew I was Jewish and I knew the basic principles of being Jewish—such as the holidays, the dietary laws, the Sabbath, and of course the disbelief of the Messiah being Jesus (with the last name Christ)—I became friendly with some men where I worked. One in particular was what you would call a "born again" Baptist. He was always *hocking* me (that means "bending my ear" in Yiddish) that I should accept Jesus as the Messiah. These guys would have their discussions and I would listen and of course become involved. Even though I didn't accept Yeshua (Hebrew for Jesus) at that time, I guess the seed was planted.

A few years later, I met this beautiful girl named Diane, fell in love with her immediately, and we got married thirteen months later (June 25, 1961). We raised two children, a boy and a girl, who grew up and got married and each had two sons. We are now the proud grandparents of four grandsons.

Prior to our son getting married, he informed me that he'd accepted Jesus as the Messiah. This was a shock to me, as it came from out of the blue. He and I had never discussed religion and since he was raised Jewish, was Bar Mitzvahed, and saw his sister getting married in the Jewish tradition, I never expected that statement coming from him. I believe I told him that this declaration came as a surprise, but I still loved him and I told him that in actuality his mother believed in Yeshua, way before I met her; she just didn't advertise it to her friends.

I then went home and gave the news to Diane. She was a little surprised, but really unconcerned because of her conclusion about Yeshua.

As a result of all this stuff, I decided to start looking into why our son and my wife accepted Yeshua. Many things were revealed to me. I had recollections of some of the old conversations I had with my prior co-workers. I had recollections of conversations I had with Diane. And most of all, I started listening to a Christian radio station to and from work. This went on for a couple years, or a bit more, and finally one day while listening to my regular church station, they began reading from the Gospel of John. The chapter and verses were 3:1–21. After hearing this, I knew that Yeshua was the Messiah and He was hated by the ruling people because of the changes He was teaching. These changes meant the end to their way of life; they would no longer be in charge. In their minds, they had to get rid of Him.

A short time after that, I decided that maybe I should try attending the congregation. Sh'mu'el Oppenheim was the interim Spiritual Leader at the time. I loved everything I was seeing and hearing.

I was so taken in by my newfound religion that I decided to get Bar Mitzvahed. You see, when I was growing up, my parents didn't think it was important for me to have a Bar Mitzvah. It wasn't that they were against it, but since I didn't want to put any effort into it they said, "Okay." Now that I felt like a newborn Jew, I wanted to have a Bar Mitzvah! So at the age of sixty-seven I read from the Torah and conducted the Shabbat Service, with the aid of a Cantor. During my speech, I publicly accepted Yeshua as my Messiah to my friends and family.

Today, I am believing even stronger that Yeshua, G-d's Son, died on that execution stake, rose from the dead and saved me from eternal death so that I can spend eternity with Hashem (Hebrew for God).

For my wife Diane, the story is a little different. She actually grew up in a predominantly Catholic suburb of New York. As a result, she had a number of non-Jewish friends and she had exposure to the Messiah (Yeshua) through the Catholic religious system. When she was twelve, she and her family moved to California, and then a few years later moved back to New York. At age fourteen, she was sent to Jewish religious studies on Sunday, where she asked so many questions about faith and practice, she was considered disruptive to the rest of the class. After we were married, we settled into the common interests of our Jewish identity, and so naturally she and I raised our kids with a Jewish upbringing.

In our household, things changed quite dramatically when we learned that our son had become a believer in Yeshua. For many years, Diane conveniently tucked away her belief in Yeshua. It was a hidden and undisclosed reality to her Jewish friends and family. But now that our son was openly discussing a relationship with the Messiah, her own beliefs and need for open relationship with Yeshua came to the surface.

After we became involved in our congregation, we introduced Diane's parents to our newfound faith. Diane's mother was ill but loved to attend the services and fellowship with the people. Her father became a believer in Yeshua and attended many of the festivals with us. As he advanced in years, he moved into an assisted living facility and attended religious services three times a week.

Today, Yeshua is one of Diane's favorite subjects to talk about, and she continues to grow in her faith and knowledge.

Aaron and Diane love the L-rd and celebrate their heritage in Judaism more today than at any other time in their past history. In retirement, they remain committed and involved to tell others what they know to be true about Yeshua.

Note specific to Judaism: when a Jewish person believes in and receives Jesus ("Yeshua" in Hebrew) as their Messiah, they refer to themselves as Messianic Jews, rather than Christians. Based on the five essentials for the Christian Faith, Christians recognize these believers as brothers and sisters in the same faith.

Buddhism: An Intellectual's Journey

Madeline Haydon was raised in the Vietnamese tradition, but came to question the practice of Buddhism because of the observance of her mother's life and her passing.

My mom, a faithful Buddhist, died in 2002. She was sixty-two. The preparations for her death are what started me really thinking and questioning the Buddhist faith we grew up in. To be fair, some of this is interwoven in the Vietnamese culture, so it's hard to divide the religion from the culture.

The seven days after someone dies is a critical time period for the soul of the deceased. We had to pay thousands of extra dollars to have twenty-four- hour access to my mother's body at the funeral home in order for us to keep a candle lit by her body in the casket (to light the way for her soul as she travels through the spirit world), and to burn incense to protect her spirit from other spirits/demons as she travels. My brothers and sisters took shifts in pairs so one of us could sleep and the other make sure the candle and incense never went out. I started wondering what if someone had one only child or no children or a spouse to do this for them? Would their spirit really be dependent on the actions of others?

Then the day of her funeral came. My dad was exceptionally nervous, fearing that enough people wouldn't show up for my mom's funeral. This is also very important, because many people attending to show their respect and mourn the passing is evidence that the deceased was a good person. I started thinking. When did my mom's soul become so dependent on other people's actions? And how stupid it was that how she lived life would be signified by a seeming popularity contest at her funeral.

My mom, a vegetarian for religious reasons, never failed in her nightly tradition of her incense and prayers. I felt all the years of her actions were reduced by the failures and actions of others. At minimum, that seemed so unfair to me...at maximum, that made no sense. You should be judged entirely on yourself.

I started looking at Christianity. I had many Christian friends. I started to weigh the hard-to-believe miracles of both religions that I never totally believed before.

As a Buddhist, I would bristle when people espoused the morality of Christians. I would counter that it's not like Buddhism advocates killing and stealing. In fact, Buddhists highly regard kindness toward others. Buddhism doesn't even want the killing of animals! Christianity isn't the only religion that teaches a moral framework.

I got into a debate with my dear Christian friend about science. I was doubtful about Noah's Ark and the Great Flood. She said they had found fossils of sea shells on top of mountains. I fired back that it was plate tectonics and the glaciers melting that carved out the Grand Canyon and could account for the fossils. Some years later, I asked her how she refutes the science of the hominids (ape-like creatures some claim to be early man), because Adam and Eve were *Homo sapiens.* She said that she believes they are just another animal form, like other primates. She said that the Bible and Genesis was not meant to be an exhaustive account of all that God created, thus orangutans were not mentioned, but they were created by Him. I thought she was shielding her eyes, blocking out reason by ignoring important pieces of science, yet I have read that many scientists say they see the fingerprints of God everywhere. With my own interest in science, I continued questioning matters of faith.

I couldn't deny that I have felt God patiently waiting for me in my subconscious. Never pushy—just there, waiting for me (in a non-creepy way). I started going to an Alpha Course (a practical introduction to the Christian faith). I read *A Case for Christ.* I heard about C. S. Lewis too. Both authors were atheists who became convinced of the Christian faith. By this time, I attended church with my in-laws, and heard the pastor explain how he too was an atheist and now he is a pastor. I had to learn more.

I met with the pastor, who walked me through the Bible from a skeptic's perspective. Why would the angel appear to women at Jesus' tomb when women were not considered credible witnesses? And if Jesus wasn't truly raised from the dead, why would any of the apostles and other followers of Jesus subject themselves to imprisonment, torture, and death for something they weren't absolutely certain of? He showed me how the Bible has endured for so many centuries, and he shared much more.

Where I once thought that Christians are uneducated and never questioned what they believed, with the pastor's help, my intellectual side was appeased. I now had to understand the spiritual aspects of the faith. My philosophy teacher in college told us whenever we want to engage in a quest for the truth, try and refute it. What remains is the truth. This is how I continued seeking.

When my husband was offered a new job, we moved to Southern California, away from all family and friends. We found a church that has really been a source of new friends as well as place of learning—without which I wouldn't be where I am in my faith journey.

In the process, I realized a lot of things about myself. I worked on forgiveness—forgiving others who'd deeply disappointed me. Once I worked on forgiveness, one of the main tenets of Christianity, my marriage was reborn, which I gratefully attribute to God.

I'm still "coming out" in my faith with my family. Some have been neutral, and others have been disappointed and see it as a signal that I've turned away from my culture and heritage, but I know that the only way to the Father is through the Son.

Madeline, her husband, and her daughter have faced many difficulties, including the long ordeal of trying to have another baby, only to lose it during pregnancy. But Madeline shares that even in that difficult experience she has an unquestionable reassuring comfort from Christ that she never knew before.

Hinduism: From Thousands of Gods to One Reconsidered

Rev. Dr. Balaji Varadarajan is a man living in India who was raised Hindu but today is an amazing Christian pastor.

I was the first son in my family, so my dad named me after the Hindu god Balaji. This was the primary Hindu god that my father and our family worshiped.

My father was a government official and an astrologist who believed from his readings that his lifespan would be thirty-six and one-half years. Trying to lengthen his life, he enlisted in many Hindu pilgrim centers, believing that the gods could add more time to his life.

He got to know a co-worker named Julie, whom we called Aunty. My father told her that he believed if he lived beyond thirty-six and one-half years, it would be because of his Hindu gods. Hearing his belief and fears, Aunty gave my dad a Bible and told him that Jesus Christ was the one true God who could answer his prayers and add years to his life.

My dad didn't believe Aunty. Instead, he said, "Let me try adding years to my life my own way through my own gods. If time permits before I die, I will also prove to you that the Bible is not a holy book. I will read this book and prove it is only my Hindu god that is a true god, and I will prove that Jesus is only a man—a good man—but he's not a god. I will prove all this before I die."

Throughout his adult life, my dad started every day by getting up at three thirty in the morning, and he followed a specific routine. First, he'd take a bath in cold water. Then he would kneel down with his eyes closed before the Hindu gods, where he would recite many chants and slogans. As the oldest son, my dad wanted me to be dedicated to his god, so he got me up every morning to sit beside him and to say the chants with him. As I followed along in the one-hundred-page book of chants, I discovered that he knew them all by heart.

With his conversation with Aunty, he added reading the Bible to his daily routine because he wanted to find something false in it, so he could disprove it. He would kneel before the Hindu gods and read the Bible aloud. He hoped his Hindu god would prove that the Bible is not true and that Jesus Christ was only a good man and not a god.

By this time he was thirty-six, and he remembered that according to astrology he was supposed to die in six months. One day, he got a pain in his throat so he went for a medical check-up. Fearful that his life was ending and out of concern for his family without him, many worries and anxious thoughts swirled around in his mind. Now he was reading the Bible around the clock—at the office, during lunch and tea time, before bed, in the morning—whenever he found time, he read.

One night, my father fell asleep with the Bible on his chest. While asleep, he had a vision. His uncle, who had already died, came to him and took him to a graveyard near the village in his hometown. Just before going through the main entrance to the graveyard, Jesus Christ appeared to my father. Christ took my dad by the right hand and separated him from his uncle. Jesus sent his uncle back into the graveyard, but He sent my dad into the village.

There's a strong Hindu belief that if a dead man comes into a living man's dream and takes him along holding his hand, it shows the living man is soon to die.

Suddenly, my father woke up with a myriad of questions. Why would Jesus Christ come into my dream? In what way am I connected with Christ? Why did Balaji not come instead? Why did I have this dream? Why is my uncle taking me to the graveyard? Why is Christ sending me to the village? As the questions filled his mind, he suddenly noticed that the boil in his throat had disappeared and the pain was gone. This made him have more questions. Why did Christ come now and give me life? Why didn't my own god come into my dream to save me?

The very next day he went for a medical exam. The doctor was amazed and told him, "I don't know what's going on here, but a divine healing has taken place in your body." The same day he went to a Christian church near our house and told the pastor what had happened. From that day on, my father totally left his Hindu gods and started worshiping Jesus Christ only.

This upset my mother greatly because of the strength of religious traditions in our family. We are from a family of priests, and my grandfather is the priest at the temple in my home village. My mother angrily warned my father, "We are from a priest family. You cannot just leave Hinduism and get into Christianity. Christianity is a foreign religion…a foreign god. If you do something like this, pretty soon a Hindu god is going to punish us."

To try to make peace, my father continued to get up at three thirty every morning and kneel before the Hindu god, but instead of worshipping the Hindu god, he secretly worshipped Jesus and read the Bible. This went on for two years.

During those years, our family life was horrible because I was caught in the middle. My dad tried to get me to go to church and read the Bible with him. My mom pleaded with me that as the first son of the family, I had to worship her gods. My mother often expressed great upset and was angry with my father. They both spewed upset on me because I wasn't following their beliefs. I became very confused and caught in the middle so frequently that those days were nearly unbearable in our home.

Two years after my dad placed his faith in Christ, my mother was having one of her fits of rage, even throwing things and breaking them, declaring, "the Hindu gods are going to punish you! You're leaving your tradition and culture and going to some foreign religion. Our god is getting angry and going to curse you!" It was a terrible night, and after much fighting, we all finally went to bed.

That very night, my mother had a dream. Two angels with big swords came to our house and took all the Hindu idols, pictures, and vessels used for the sacrifices, and put them in a bag and threw the bag on my mother's leg. They flashed the sword in front of her and said angrily, "Do not worship any of these evil angels any more. Do not worship Hindu gods any more. Just worship Christ!"

My mother woke terrified and frantically woke all of us up to help her gather all the idols and religious items. We put them in many sacks and threw them outside the home. No one knew what to think.

Early the next morning, we put all our Hindu books in a heap— books worth a lot of money—and burned them because my father did not want anyone else to pick them up and read them ever again. The rest of the items we threw off a bridge into the ocean.

Some days later, my mother attended church with my father. The visiting pastor was one of the great Christian speakers, Justin Prabakan. He knew my father's story and had been praying for us. Learning that my mother was in attendance, he said, "I heard my friend's wife has come to the church today. Can I see her? Can she raise a hand or stand so we can pray for her?" Most uncomfortably, my mother stood up and was prayed for. After that day, she joined the faith of my father.

Two years later, when I was eighteen, I too put my faith in Christ. One day when I was in church, a man from Singapore was sharing the Word of God, and he said, "I sense the spirit of God moving here and there are a few people He has chosen for a calling of full-time ministry. I want to pray for them." I was standing in the back of the church, feeling very shy, afraid to go forward, but I knew in my heart that God was calling me. The man kept asking for people to come forward. Then I felt a big hand whack me on the back. This was strange because I was resting against the wall. Then before I knew it I was at the front of the church. As soon as I came forward, the man said, "Okay, everybody's here. Let's pray for these people."

Not too long after, I went to Bible college to prepare for full-time ministry. For three years, I worked toward my bachelor of theology degree while working as an associate pastor for two years. I then was given an assignment from the Bible college to start a church in a Hindu village.

In 1994, after I'd completed Bible college, I served as a pastor in Thirunallar, where the one and only Saturn Temple is located. This is the temple that Hindus from all over the world come to so that they can be cleansed, if they are Saturn worshipers. It's such a big temple that when prime ministers of India and cabinet ministers are sworn in, they come to the temple's secret gate, worship there, then return home to start their term of office. It's an important pilgrimage place for Hindus around the globe.

No one is allowed to start any churches in this area because of the Hindu reverence for their Saturn god. In fact, Hindus had destroyed the nearby big Roman Catholic church, but, because of all I'd seen Christ do for my family, I pressed past the fear.

What followed were months and months of difficulties. The Hindu priest of the Saturn Temple called me one morning and threatened me. He told me I could not start a church any closer than six kilometers away from the temple. His phone call was full of all sorts of threats, and he hung up furious. From that day on, the people from the Saturn Temple gave me trouble. I was no longer allowed to eat at the hotel where I normally took my meals. At night, they would come and knock on my door to see if I was home with intent of harming me. Three times they tried to kill me.

To get out of danger, I began leaving after church on Sundays, making a seven-hour trip to Chennai. One night, while I was gone, they broke into my home and broke the fan and burned the Bibles. When I returned, they told me they did this while I was gone, but next time, they would do it while I was there.

I called my dad, who tried to put some pressure on the Thirunallar police. They would not listen to my complaint about the break-in and damage because the Hindu people had influenced them. I didn't ever get help from the police, but help did come when one of the men who'd been threatening me accepted Christ.

For six months, not one person visited my church. Every day I went door to door, riding my bicycle at least forty kilometers to tell people about Jesus Christ and invite them to my church.

All alone in my house on Sundays, I still worshiped for two hours. Nobody was there, but I could pray anyway for the cobras to stay out of my house, and for the people. Neighbors and people walking by heard me preaching to an empty house or singing from my hymn books.

My sponsoring church gave me enough money for rent, but not for my daily provisions. The Lord provided my food and everything I needed.

One day, a Christian lady was transferred to the city to work in the local bank. She showed up one Sunday morning to an empty church-house full of open hymn books and she sat down to worship. She stayed and worshiped, and at the end, explained that she'd heard of my difficulties. She encouraged me to hold more services, not just on Sundays.

We began meeting Saturdays, fasting and praying for the townspeople. The third week, an entire Hindu family visited the church. After the service, a woman approached me to explain that her husband was seriously sick, stating that she believed he'd been engaged in witchcraft. She explained his dreadful condition and told me he's been getting worse and worse over the last fifteen years. I stopped to pray for her. Within minutes, her daughter ran into the room exclaiming that her daddy had been experiencing relief for the past forty minutes and his stomach had gone down to normal size! We ultimately learned that the younger brother was jealous of the woman's husband. Some fifteen years earlier he had called on a Hindu priest and had a curse put on his older brother. Our prayers and fasting broke the stronghold and that very day everyone except the younger brother put their faith in Christ. Before I left town, sixteen whole families including their children believed in Jesus Christ as their Savior. This is very rare in India. All the families continued following Christ after I left.

Pastor Balaji continues to work with various organizations doing ministry, children's ministry, teacher training, literacy programs, and working with slum dwellers in Chennai. Most recently, he has started a full-time ministry in a rural village. He has a church and hopes to build a children's home and a training center for others to be equipped to go into full-time ministry. In addition, he has plans to establish a research center on Christian studies with the recognition of the

University Grants Commission India. India is known for its research centers for individual persons like Mahatma Gandhi, Annadurai, and Dr. Ambedkar, and for Hinduism and Islam, and asks, "Why not also for Christian studies?" He plans to undertake this mission as soon as he completes his Ph.D.

New Age: Old Deception

Moira Noonan is one who escaped the New Age movement and who now spends her efforts warning people of its deception. Here's her story.

My mother sent us (my brothers and sisters) to Catholic school so the nuns could raise us, explaining that she believed they did a better job than she could. The first school I went to was in Detroit for kindergarten, a Sacred Heart Convent School in the order of St. Madeline Sophie. By the time I was in third grade, we had moved from Detroit to New Jersey, where I attended public school because there was no Catholic school in that area. By eighth grade, I was sent away to boarding school in Philadelphia called Eden Hall, the Sacred Heart Convent. When I was in tenth grade, the school suffered a fire and burned down.

I was transferred to a secular college prep boarding school called MacDuffie School for Girls. This transition placed a real damper on my faith formation. This very secular and non-Christian environment started me out on the dangerous path into the New Age world. One of my teachers, in her twenties, had befriended me and many of the girls at the school both during and after school hours. She studied in India and had a strong belief in the Hindu religion. She was also engaged to a Hindu professor at Princeton University. He wore the traditional dress of a turban and came to visit her at our boarding school on a regular basis. We attended many different Indian concerts, including

Ravi Shankar, and became more fascinated with the mystery of the Indian culture and religion. Additionally, some of us were taken to Indian restaurants in attempt to immerse us in all that was Indian.

By the time I graduated from high school, I was convinced I needed to be enlightened and go to India and find my guru, "my living teacher to show me the way to God." After graduation, I decided to attend college in Colorado and attended both the University of Denver and the Colorado University. I had always had the idea that one day I would go to India—the seed of this new religious belief had been planted into me. I found fascination with the gurus who came to the campuses, offering students Eastern meditations and *satsang* sessions with them. Some of them initiated us with the Third Eye initiation, and we thought we were that much closer to Nirvana—an enlightened state.

It is a common belief among many New Agers that a guru needs to be alive (as opposed to channeling help) in order to help you reach Nirvana. The Rashneesh Movement was one of the more aggressive movements on the college campus I attended. This movement really took off and their guru eventually moved from India to the West Coast in the United States to be with all of the young followers and to set up communes, basically creating a cult following.

By my junior year of college, I had transferred to the University of Washington in Seattle. Deciding to do a semester abroad, I attended college in Avignon, France. While I was in France I traveled to Greece and Turkey, and thought I'd take a train to India because I didn't feel the need to finish college. The concept of being enlightened overpowered my need to finish my education. However, my grandmother tracked me down and convinced me to come home and finish school, so I graduated from college with my degree from the University of Washington.

During this time, the media and wildly popular celebrities, such as the Beatles, were following gurus and promoting guru worship. They ended up with Maharishi Yogi, the founder of Transcendental Meditation, which became a worldwide attraction, crossing many cultural barriers because of the Beatles' popularity. This increased my attraction to the Hindu and Eastern religions. I was intent on finding a guru in order attain enlightenment, especially considering the New Age belief in reincarnation.

However, the feminist movement and the attitude that women were nothing without a career greatly impacted me. Once again, I put India on the back shelf to enter the career path, to become a successful publisher. I focused solely on my work and had no time for spiritual matters.

By the age of twenty-eight, I had accomplished my goal of being a publisher and was thriving—working in Hawaii with Visitor Publications, Inc. Unfortunately, at age thirty, I was in a major auto accident. The accident left me seriously disabled. I could not work or drive, and was in constant pain. Searching for a way to relieve the pain, I turned back to the New Age movement for help.

My insurance company sent me to Dr. Norman Shelly's Pain and Rehabilitation Clinic in La Crosse, Wisconsin, which was one of the first model pain clinics in the country (now incorporated into the Menninger Clinic in the Midwest). The main training in this clinic was called autogenic training, which was a combination of hypnosis and New Thought philosophy. The New Thought belief comes from the Science of the Mind, created by Dr. Ernest Holmes of the Theosophical Society and Mary Baker Eddy, who founded the Christian Science religion. During my stay at the pain clinic, we as patients were placed in subliminal mode to alter our brain waves to alter our thinking, while feeding the brain subliminal messages of a new belief system with new values attached, a "mind over matter: way to become pain free. "If you believe you have no pain, then you have no pain." The staff at the clinic actually verbally denied any form of suffering and refuted the prospect of virtue in suffering. They firmly believed suffering was a result of our own guilt. They told us that waiting for help from a Savior was hopeless, and if we wanted to be pain-free, we needed to do it ourselves. The remedy of being free from suffering, to be healed or pain-free, must come from the self within. The New Age belief is that the self is divine and therefore can heal itself.

These subliminally transmitted auto-suggestions were conducted hourly, each day and night, while we were sleeping, for the duration of my stay, until we were hypnotized with the messages. I stayed at the pain clinic for about a month. When I left the clinic, they gave me books and tapes, a headphone set, and sleep pillow headphones to take home so I could stay on the autogenic system in order to stay pain-free. They said I needed to keep this "New Thought" in my mind to reinforce my new way of thinking. All of this was actually a mental reprogramming of any Christian value system left in me.

The professional therapists at the pain clinic told us that if we wanted to stay pain-free, we needed to go to New Age churches, not Christian churches. They emphasized that only the New Age churches would support our new values and keep us pain-free, and that if we went back to the Christian churches, we would feel guilty and experience pain again.

Wanting to stay pain-free, of course, I followed their lead and started out at Unity churches which are now New Age. I eventually ended up joining the ministry training program at the North County Church of Religious Science in Encinitas, California, and spent four years learning under a former Catholic who was the minister. The in-depth "New Thought" continued until I truly had a new belief system.

The texts, *A Course in Miracles* and *The Science of the Mind,* were the main texts for teaching us "New Thought."

I became a prayer practitioner at the Seaside Church of Religious Science in Del Mar, California, where we did prayer treatment with people one on one. From there, I started learning New Age occult healing arts and I became certified as a Reiki healer and master trainer, as well as trained in "Hands of Light" training by the Barbara Brennar School of Healing. These forms of occult healing arts use spirit guides, which are, in reality, fallen angels or demons. I did not realize this at the time, and neither did I realize the spiritual dangers I was falling prey to. During the prayer practitioner work at the churches, we assisted people in manifesting their desires, using God more like a genie who grants you wishes. The essence of the New Age teachings is that each of us is a "god," so by exercise of our divine will, we can manifest our desires into human experience.

I later met Anthony Robbins of Robbins Research, San Diego, and followed his fire walking programs and his Neuro-Linguistic Programming (NLP) trainings, which led me to become certified in NLP. From that training I continued on to study hypnosis. In 1989, I became a certified Ericksonian hypnotherapist. The emphasis was two-part: past life regression therapy and future life progression therapy. New Age espouses reincarnation, so this therapy of exploring former lives to help direct the future is significant. Dr. Milton Erickson, former professor of the University of Arizona, designed Ericksonian hypnotherapy, a specific style of hypnosis. As I became further immersed in the world of hypnosis, along with all that preceded, the process became a complete reprogramming of my mind, and resulted in a serious loss of personal willpower.

The beginning of my conversion started in 1990. While in Hawaii at an Advanced Regression/Progression Therapy training, I was resting in the lounge between classes, reading an article about the New Age leader and teacher Sandra Ray's trip to Medjugorje in Bosnia-Herzegovina. Sandra's aim in going was to visit "Mother Mary." She said she was invited by the priest at St. James Church to be in the room with the visionaries during the apparition. Her experience there gave her the insight to start the goddess movement, which is very big within the New Age. She believed she witnessed the heaven goddess, "Mother Mary," coming down to meet the earth goddess, Gaia. In reading this article, what really struck me was that I knew Mother Mary was definitely not a goddess—she was a human being. There was a shred of truth left from my early childhood instruction from the nuns of Sacred Heart reminding me of the fact that Mary was truly human and was also the mother of Jesus. This introspection caused me to immediately question what I'd been taught in the New Age movement.

When I returned home to San Diego, I happened upon a *Life* magazine with a picture of a statue of our Lady (Mother Mary) on the cover with the caption, "Do you believe in Miracles?" I bought it as a follow-up to the New Age magazine I had read while in Hawaii. I read the magazine cover to cover to see if they called her a goddess too and was relieved to find out they did not. The testimonies in *Life* magazine were beginning to evangelize me as I read true life stories of meetings and miracles with the intervention of supernatural grace from heaven for people all over the world. I realized I could be one of those persons too, and I became exceedingly hungry for the truth.

By divine providence, I next met a woman on the street in La Jolla, California, named Beverly Nelson, a Lay Missionary of Charity in the order of Mother Theresa—a key person I believe the Lord put in my life to help me out of the brainwashed deception I'd embraced. I actually did not realize that my soul was in a battle or that I'd sold out to the demonic world as a New Age occult therapist. Beverly was a prayer warrior and intercessor who began praying over the battle for my eternal life. Once she and her Bible study group began praying for me to be released from the New Age, I began feeling serious conviction to stop all New Age practices. Beverly spoke to me and shared truth with such sweetness and sureness that I eventually followed her to meet Mother Teresa and her nuns, and we joined them in prayer at their chapel. The peace I experienced while there was not of this world and I came to find the peace of the Lord Jesus and to experience Him as the Prince of Peace.

As a result of Beverly's encouragement, I joined the Lay Missionaries of Charity, and became active as a missionary myself serving the poor in Tijuana and San Diego. I joined the Rite of Christian Initiation for Adults, a formation class to initiate former Catholics back into the faith, at St. Francis Church in Vista, California. I became a sponsor for many of my New Age friends to realize the truth that would also set them free. Among those were a former New Age doctor, my former New Age teacher, a top New Age musician, and many personal friends who had been in New Age for over thirty years. The grace of God was with all of us, convicting us with a desire for conversion to find life in Christ—the Truth and the Light of the Way. We were all ransomed from darkness into His marvelous light! Colossians 1:13–14: "For He has rescued us from the kingdom of darkness and transferred us into the Kingdom of His dear Son, who purchased our freedom and forgave our sins" (NLT).

Moira Noonan is devoted to writing and speaking to warn people that the New Age movement is seductively dangerous.[2] It is the same attractive lie that Satan gave to Eve in the Garden of Eden—that we can be enlightened beyond what God offers and become like God. The belief that there's no need to submit to God's will because we are each our own God appeals to the natural pride of man. She cautions, "The Selfism that New Age teaches eventually leads to Satan, the enemy of God, who seeks to destroy our souls."

Islam: A Struggle within the Struggle

What follows is Safi's story. His last name is intentionally withheld for his safety.

I grew up in a small farming village in Iran. After high school in 1976, I came to the United States for college education. As I grew up, my understanding of Allah was like this:

1. When I was eight years old, one day as I was walking with my classmates back to school for the afternoon, I remembered I had not done my Muslim noon prayers, and so I told my classmates to go on and I would catch up later after I went back home to do my prayers. We usually got to school a little earlier and played in school yard before class started. My friends, they did not want me to leave, so they told me I was wasting my time with prayers. I went and told my father that and he explained to me if there is God, I would be accepted in heaven. But if there was no God, I would get some exercise. This was my father's way to say it's better to pray. But even at that young age, prayer wasn't enough for me. I wish my father could offer more certainty about why a person prays, especially with never being sure if we were good enough. From childhood, I was told that Jihad mean going to war for Islam. In fact, they told me one day all Muslims will kill all non-Muslims, starting from their own home, and that is the last and the true Jihad.

2. When I was eighteen years old, I was questioning the existence of God. As a teen with a life away from home, I had many problems: school, lack of friends, etc. I thought to myself, *If this is all there is to life, I do not want to continue.* From fertilizer (dust) to fertilizer (dust) was not enough for me. One late evening before going to sleep, I

was lying on a summer bed in the balcony and watching the sky. The moon was out and there was a small cloud in the sky. In my desperation, I asked if there was God, would He show me by turning that cloud into rain. I fell asleep and minutes later my hands got wet and I woke up to see the cloud gone. I knew in my deepest heart that God had made it rain in response to my cry. I share this so you can see the Muslim mind: (A) There is no solid relationship with Allah; (B) The small relationship there is, is based on cause and effect—waiting for God to show Himself. When I started school at South Dakota State University, I wanted to be a doctor. In my mind, I was still godless and even started studying about Communism—reading books by Ho-chi Minh, Marx, and Lenin. My Iranian friends and I were often invited to community programs designed for international students. In these programs, I met friends who were Christians.

My Christian friends would tell me about Jesus. They believed He is God's Son. As a Muslim, I believed He is a prophet. I would tell them Jesus was the love side of God and Moses was the judgment and anger of God. Muhammad combined the two for a more perfect religion. I thought Christians were too prideful to say they are destined for heaven. Muhammad had the last revelation of God.

Meanwhile, I was learning about how Jesus lived, which was very different than I'd been taught. Little by little, I learned He was a very smart man. I learned of how He placed God above man's thought life. For example, He said when you think about adultery, you are guilty of the same. Who but the true God would know my thoughts? He eliminated the sin from the start, beginning from the mind where things are planned (cut the sin from its root). I learned to respect Him highly because He died for what He believed.

I was a member of the Muslim Student Association, so when Iran's leader, Ayatollah Ali Khamenei, went to Iran, I also left to go. Based on my upbringing, I wanted to serve under him in the Revolutionary Guard. Through some miracles, like not being able to find the draft office, I ended up back in the United States.

Two years later, when I was finished with school, I was trying to find out if I must go back to Iran. I asked my family to see what they would advise. As a Muslim, I would listen to my family. Some said stay because there was a war with Iraq, and some said come. I did not get any word from my father, whom I would have obeyed absolutely. Since I didn't get any solid advice, I looked to the Koran (Muslims' holy book) for direction. I was about to open my Koran and see what the page I opened it to said. If it designated good, I would go, and if bad, I would stay. This is how Koran pages are marked: at the corner of each page there is a word, "good" or "bad" in a parenthesis, and this is commonly used by Muslims to make decisions. I decided I could not trust this method, so I read the Koran instead and maybe God would show me what to do. Muslims normally don't read the Koran, and they believe you must be a scholar to understand it, so they rather listen to the Mullah's description of the Koran. I have a word-to-word translation of Koran in both Arabic (original form) and Persian. I was reading from the beginning *surah Baghareh,* verses 86–87. It says God gave Moses the *Tura* (Old Testament) and Muhammad the Koran and Jesus the Holy Spirit.

Here I forgot about my decision problem and started thinking about who Jesus is and why He got the Holy Spirit while Moses and Muhammad each got a book. By now, I knew the Holy Spirit could make one hundred such books in a second. I also remembered that the Koran said Jesus is born of the Virgin Mary, conceived by the Holy Spirit, and if anyone says Mary became pregnant by her later husband Joseph, it is a blasphemy. So my question was, "Whose son is Jesus?" The Koran strangely calls Him Son of Mary. But what Muslim has ever been named after the mother? So that night (Tuesday), I asked God to show me who is Jesus, and I slept.

The next morning, I got up with a very good feeling. It was like a person with a house mortgage of thirty years who has just got a call that their mortgage was paid by someone after only five years. That morning, I understood how God prepared man all this time for His Son to be born through the Prophets. And at the perfect time, He sent Him to be born into human race and die and reconcile us to Himself and remove our sin. I understood that Jesus came from God. Therefore, He is God's Son and that is why the Koran did not designate a father for Him other than the Holy Spirit, who is God's Spirit. So I went and tried to explain it to my Iranian friends and they said it was blasphemy. So I went and told one of those pastors whom I wanted to convert to Islam that I believed Jesus is God's Son; he said I had become a Christian.

Not too long after this, I was threatened by other Muslims in Brooking, South Dakota, where I lived at the time. Khamenei had said any Muslim changing their religion must be killed and my schoolmates would show me the newspaper and tell me they would follow the order. It was frightening, but finding a vital relationship with God was of highest value to me, and I would not go back.

I went and shared the good news with other Christian friends. Now I know that I have eternal life with Jesus in heaven, according to the Bible in verse John 1:12: "Yet to all who received Him to those who believed in His name, He gave the right to become children of God." Also, I am sure there is a heaven and hell, and I'm going to heaven to live with Jesus forever because Jesus, according to the Gospel, paid for my sins. Unlike the non-relationship with Allah, relationship with God through faith in Jesus gives all meaning to life. Praise His name! I am so thankful and changed.

Safi is presently a professor at a college. He seeks to impart Christ's love to his students, by helping them understand their world through science—because as he says, "science is all God's idea."

Consider the Cost

Each person who seeks to find truth starts from their own individual path, with his or her unique family dynamics, social, historical, cultural distinctions, and more. For some, coming to faith in Jesus Christ is life-threatening. For others, it means rejection by their family and friends. Knowing this, Jesus, speaking to a great multitude, said:

> Anyone who comes to Me but refuses to let go of their father, mother, spouse, children, brothers, sisters—yes, even one's own self!—can't be my disciple. Anyone who won't shoulder his own cross and follow behind me can't be my disciple. Is there anyone here who, planning to build a new house, doesn't first sit down and figure the cost so you'll know if you can complete it? If you only get the foundation laid and then run out of money, you're going to look pretty foolish. Everyone passing by will poke fun at you; "He started something he couldn't finish." Or can you imagine a king going into battle against another king without first deciding whether it is possible with his ten thousand troops to face the twenty thousand troops of the other? And if he decides he can't, won't he send an emissary and work out a truce? Simply put, if you're not willing to take what is dearest to you, whether plans or people, and kiss it good-bye, you can't be my disciple.[3]

It takes a great deal of courage to seriously consider what you believe and why you believe it. But the courage required to believe in and receive the truth is greater still.

Chapter Twelve

Faith Perspectives on Good and Evil

The problem of evil and suffering is the central concern that makes it difficult for many people to believe in the existence of a good and loving God who is concerned with humanity.

Judaism, based on their scriptures, claims that G-d is good and loving, but Judaism's exploration and treatment of the origin and existence of evil and suffering is ambiguous. Some firmly believe that G-d did not create evil, Satan, or some other evil deity. Others, with reference to Isaiah 45:7, believe that G-d created both good and evil, stating that G-d created Evil Inclination, the angel called Satan, to tempt people to do evil. By ignoring the temptation, a person draws closer to G-d and becomes more holy; therefore, there is no conflict, but a purpose in evil. All seem to hold out that, in the end, G-d will make all things good, though ideas of how are not known. Judaism's explanation seems to hang on the premise that man will eventually choose wrong. Judaism explains that evil exists because of humanity's free-will choices and that all that happens on earth is under G-d's control, which will ultimately be for good.[1]

Islam espouses that Allah is good, and He leads the faithful into what is good yet Muslims live between the hope that Allah will be merciful and the fear that Allah will not be. There are literally many different schools of thought concerning the existance of evil as it relates to Allah. The theological school known as Mu'tazilism emphasized Allah's all-goodness, and argued that since Allah is All-Good, He cannot be the source of evil. Most believe evil arises not from Allah, but from His creations who act independent of Allah. By contrast, the Ash'arite school emphasized Allah's All-Powerfulness and argued that if He did not control all the affairs of the universe, something other than Allah could bring about things that went against His will. For them, whatever occurs had to occur because Allah willed it. Otherwise, He would be neither All-Powerful, in complete control, nor, ultimately, "God." The founder of the Traditionalist school once asked, rhetorically, "If Allah is wholly unconnected to evil, what role can He play in lifting it?" Muslims believe that in the end, evil will be conquered when Islam converts the world to Islam, and kills the Jews.[2]

In **Hinduism** evil has no real existence, being part of the illusory world of phenomena. Hinduism sees evil as part of the continuity of life. One of the main deities in Hinduism, Shiva, is both a creator and a destroyer. His consort, Kali, is the black, the destroyer of the universe, at the end of the age of Kali. Vishnu is the creator, Shiva is the destroyer, and yet Shiva, like Kali, is not necessarily feared. Rather, each is revered for their power. It is understood that all that is created, including life and this earth, must inevitably be destroyed.

With **Buddhism**, there is no particular dealing with evil. Rather, it is merely another aspect of suffering. Suffering, according to Buddhism, is a product of ignorance. Once a person is aware of oneself, then he/she will recognize that he/she is capable of evil only in ignorance. Suffering and pain can be ended through the pursuit of truth and self-knowledge.

New Age tends to deny, or at least minimize, the fundamental existence of evil. In this regard, the New Age parallels both its theological forerunner, the nineteenth century New Thought movement—a derivative of Christian Science that believes in the ultimate illusionary nature of evil.

Just reading the headline news in your local community should be enough to convince you that evil and all it brings is far more than an illusion of the mind. This leads us to reconsider good and evil in light of the prospect of a superior being—in the light of the existence of God.

The dilemma for most people, as explained by Dan Story, author of *Defending Your Faith: Reliable Answers for a New Generation of Seekers and Skeptics,* is that either God wants to prevent evil but does not have the power to do it, or He has the power to do it but does not want to. In either case, He is not a good and loving God concerned about humanity's suffering evil. The problem of evil can be reduced to the assumption that specifically the Christian God is incompatible with the world as it is.[3]

This conclusion is in error. In fact, in contrast to all other religions and philosophies, *Christianity is the one faith that best describes the presence of evil and human suffering.* Moreover Christianity offers the only possible solution to the problem of evil: redemption.[4]

Christianity's Explanation for Good and Evil

In my considered opinion, the relationship between good and evil can be best explained through Christianity. As explained in chapter ten of this book, God created man with a free will. The purpose in this is so that any loving relationship between God and man would be genuine. Beings preprogrammed to love God would not make for genuine relationship. God also made it clear to the first man, Adam, what would happen if he chose his own way rather than to remain obedient to God. Just as with any moral decision, there are either consequences or rewards. God made it clear that to disobey would mean that Adam's spirit within him would die, and he would be separated from God and all that is good. To disobey God is to reject Him.

Adam's love and allegiance was tested in the Garden of Eden, a time and place where everything God had created on earth was pure and holy. Lucifer, a created angel, who like all angels had been given free will, had previously and foolishly sought to dethrone God according to Isaiah 14:12–17—God, who is all powerful, cannot be dethroned. The consequence for Lucifer and all his evil dominions, was banishment from heaven. Indeed, about one-third of all rebellious angelic beings were banished from heaven. Lucifer became known as Satan, the father of all lies.

The book of Genesis reveals that Satan slyly disguised himself as a beguiling serpent-creature and entered the Garden of Eden intent to continue in his evil ways against God and everything God created. First, Satan enticed the woman, Eve, to disobey God. He told her that she would not die as God said she would if she ate the fruit of the Tree of Knowledge of Good and Evil. Satan went on to say that, "God knows that in the day you eat of it, your eyes will be opened and you will be like God, knowing good and evil."[5] Deceived by Satan, Eve took of the fruit and ate.

Adam, who was with his wife, clearly did not prevent Eve from disobedience—sinning against God. This, in and of itself, was an act of disobedience toward God because God had given Adam charge to protect his family.

Now realizing that the woman who was made of his side—a very part of him—was no longer like him, Adam had to choose. His options were to be forever separated from his wife whom God made from and for him, or to be separated from God, the Creator of all.

145

He chose his wife. Eve gave Adam some of the fruit and he ate. And instantly everything God had created to be holy and good became corrupted—became sin. This ushered in evil, pain suffering, and atrocities of every kind into the earth and humanity. As God warned, Adam and Eve's disobedience caused their holy, pure, and life-infused spirits—the part of them that allowed them to commune with God—to die. No longer were they able to relate with God; instead, they related with Satan. And every human being born ever since has inherited this same spiritually dead condition, unable to relate with God.

According to Christianity, sin is a condition we inherit and are accountable for as humans, once we reach the age of accountability (no longer being young children). Many take exception that we should suffer because of the act of the first man and first woman. But as the first human ever, Adam represents all humanity. He was and is the corporate head of the human race. Consider also that Adam and Eve succumbed to the deception of Satan from the position of and in an environment that was pure and holy. Often we think that we would have chosen differently, but what reason do we have to think that?

Other Views of Creation and Good and Evil

Specific to **Buddhism**, writer Angelo Caiazzo wrote: "Finding the origin of man according to Buddhism is no easy trick to perform. The very assumption that there could even *be* a beginning to the world, let alone mankind, is questionable to most Buddhists... [Buddha] would not go into a discussion of the origin of the universe. To him, gaining knowledge about such matters was a waste of time because a man's task was to liberate himself from the present, not the past or the future. It is the effort of each individual to find freedom from the cycle of life [reincarnation] through good works."[6]

Since Buddhists believe that the universe and the person do not really exist, there can be no real solution to the problem of evil because all is an illusion.

Different creation stories and Creator personalities exist side-by-side in **Hinduism**. One story explains that Brahma's first human creations were saints who, immediately upon being created, fell into deep meditation, finding no rest in the things of the world. Thus the Brahma saw no possibility of propagation of their species. While he was meditating on what course he should pursue, his own form divided itself, one half becoming man and the other half becoming woman. From these sprang all humanity. Concerning the nature of man, numerous theories are found in Hinduism; the most common follows: Man is made up of five (some say seven) "sheaths" or bodies in which the *atman* (God within) is the true self is contained, the part of man that passes from one life to the next toward perfection and freedom by way of reincarnation and through good works.[7]

The Hindu view does not explain where evil came from, nor does it account for any conclusion of evil entirely—just potentially for the individual who achieves enlightenment. And though there are hundreds of gods in Hinduism, not one is able to resolve the existence of evil.

New Age, like Buddhism, doesn't seem to have any reason to seek to know the origin of creation, and has a vast description about the nature of man, with the recognition of God in everything, including the self. It would be difficult for New Agers to clearly define the origin of man or evil, because "New Age draws its practices and philosophies and sometimes inspiration from major world religions: Buddhism, Taoism, Chinese folk religion, Christianity, Hinduism, Islam, Judaism, Sikhism, with strong influences from East Asian religions, Gnosticism, Neopaganism, New Thought, Spiritualism, Theosophy, Universalism, and Western esotericism. The term *New Age* refers to the coming astrological Age of Aquarius."[8]

Secular humanism and **New Age** suppose that everything is a function of random material processes and thus they deny, or at least minimize, the fundamental existence of good and evil.

Additional Explanations of Evil

Some people groups believe that evil is a force independent of God—a being or force that exists beyond God, over whom God has no control. This would mean that there are two opposing matters presumably of equal power—in effect, two gods,—and that would mean that there can be no end to evil, pain, and suffering.

Some purport that ignorance is the source of evil—that humanity is ignorant of the right choices to make. Therefore, higher knowledge is needed to make right choices. This would place individuals such as Buddha, Muhammad, Dr. Helen Schucman (author of *A Course in Miracles*), Marianne Williamson, and Neale Donald Walsch, the modern day leaders of New Age, as those more enlightened and able to guide others into right choices.

Atheists tend to promote the idea the evil is relative, that only cultures or individuals decide what is right and wrong—that no universal standard exists, but even the atheists don't live within their own definition. Atheists will claim that murder, stealing, and rape are wrong for everyone. This is inconsistent with their claim that cultures or individuals determine what is evil.

Buddhism, New Age, and other Eastern religions and philosophies believe that evil and suffering are but illusions. This ignores or denies the problem of evil, rather than dealing with it. Pain and suffering exist. To deny their existence is not reality, but is in actuality operating under delusion.

None of the faiths, except **Christianity** and **Judaism**, see humanity as the cause of ushering in pain and suffering to this world; neither do the other religions describe mankind as having disobeyed God.

All but Christianity believe that redemption from the suffering of this world is achieved from each individual's specific good works—Judaism is no exception. Christianity believes that there is nothing man can do to help himself—man needs someone greater to deliver humankind from evil, pain, and suffering.

The biblical account of the origin and nature of mankind and how sin ushered in evil, pain, and suffering through Adam, in contrast to the explanations, if any, given by other religious faith or philosophy, provides the most comprehensive and plausible explanation. The Christian belief is that God is sovereign over all, which is not the same as God being responsible for all. God is nothing but pure and holy. Evil exists separate from Him, born out of free-will choice.

Christianity Is About Relationship, Not Religion

The character of God, as recognized by Christians, is good and holy. As such, He cannot not create evil. With foreknowledge, He provided free will, aware that choice for evil could and would result. However, we must also understand that God's knowing all things does not mean that God determines all things. God knew He had the wisdom and power to overcome evil. His heart is to draw those who desire relationship with Him, to Himself, which He's been doing since the original fall of man.

Still, many ask, "If God is good, loving, and merciful, why does He allow evil, pain, and suffering to continue? Why hasn't He simply overcome it?" He has overcome it. With foreknowledge, God knew

149

what would happen, and He devised a plan to overcome the problem of evil, pain, and suffering. He devised a plan to eradicate the existence of sin. His solution is at work—now.

It was not God's preference that Lucifer rebel. It was Lucifer's choice. It was not God's preference that Adam and Eve rebel. It was their own choice. God knew what would happen before it did. Yet, He continued on in His sovereignty, wisdom, and power with His plan for creation and working sin out. He is not "working sin out" in the sense that it is difficult for Him. Rather, according to His perfect time table with the beginning and the end of all time and humanity in His view, He is actively working it out.

Author Dan Story states it this way: "The key to understanding why God allows the consequences of evil to continue is bound up with human freedom. God created every human ever born to worship, obey and have fellowship with Him—love Him. Genuine love is inseparable from free-will. God wanted Adam to show his love by freely choosing obedience."[9]

To have programmed man to love God would not produce genuine love. Free will is absolutely necessary for a genuine loving relationship. With free will, there is always the chance that humanity will make the wrong choice. This prospect was no surprise to God. From His love for humanity, in His wisdom and power, God determined it was better to allow the presence of evil to ultimately work out the best of all possible worlds—one that has experienced evil, and, as a result, willfully chooses to turn from it.

Understanding Genesis

I hope you agree that the most complete explanation for the existence of evil, pain, and suffering is found in the Christian interpretation of the Old Testament. Justice would have been served if God left humanity in its fallen state, but it would not be expressing His love. As soon as Adam and Eve admitted their disobedience, which in itself is an act of acknowledging God as supreme, God responded. Speaking to Satan, God said:

> Because you have done this, you are cursed more than all cattle, and more than every beast of the field, on your belly you shall go, and you shall eat dust all the days of your life. And I will put enmity between you and the woman and between your seed and her Seed; he shall bruise your head and you shall bruise his heel...[10]

To the woman God said, "I will greatly multiply your sorrow and your conception; in pain you shall bring forth children; your desire shall be for your husband, and he shall rule over you."[11]

Then to Adam He said: "Because you have heeded the voice of your wife, and have eaten from the tree of which I commanded you, saying, 'You shall not eat of it, cursed is the ground for your sake; in toil you shall eat of it all the days of your life. Both thorns and thistles it shall bring forth for you, and you shall eat the herb of the field. In the sweat of your face, you shall eat bread till you return to the ground, for out of it you were taken; for dust you are, and to dust you shall return."[12]

God first cursed Satan more than any other creature. He next declared that He would put enmity between Satan and the woman; more specifically, between his seed and her seed. This declaration is considered the first promise that God would personally provide a Redeemer to deliver humanity out of the ravages of sin and all the pain, suffering, and death it brings.

Since Adam and Eve had already eaten of the Tree of Knowledge of Good and Evil, God banished them from the Garden. This was to prevent them from eating of the Tree of Life, for had they done so, they would have lived forever in their fallen state.

This story about the origin of creation, the entrance of sin to the world and God's response reveals He is a compassionate, merciful, and loving God. He does not want to be separated from any one of His creatures, but neither will He impose or force Himself on anyone. Just as it was the individual willful decisions of Adam and Eve to reject God, so ever since God has permitted every individual to willfully receive Him or not. All through the history of humanity, as described in the Old Testament and sufficiently confirmed through archeology and other extra-biblical evidence, God has continued to work to fulfill His promise for those who want His redemption.

God has continued to be personally involved in the affairs of humanity to this day, protecting us from evil and ourselves. So far, He's withheld the punishment we deserve. But the Bible is clear that punishment will come. Rather than condemning God for allowing evil, we should be thankful He withholds the punishment we deserve. Dan Story helps provide perspective:

> God has taken steps to prevent evil from running amok. He has implemented measures that prevent fallen man from literally destroying himself. God institutionalized governments to control lawlessness and promote social order; marriage to control sexual diseases; moral standards to guide interrelationships of people, and the church to restrain evil by acting as a light of spiritual truth. Most importantly, God works to prevent Satan from having full rule over this earth.[13]

In all other faiths, man must earn entrance into heaven, Nirvana, the next life, to please God, and so on. However, the God of the Christian faith reveals there is nothing we can do to earn a place in heaven. It is a gift to be received from God.

Chapter Thirteen

The Different Views of Jesus

The Jewish, Muslim, and Christian faiths all acknowledge Jesus as an historical figure, though each group views Him very differently.

Judaism recognizes Jesus as a Jewish man from Nazareth who was hung on a cross the Day of Preparation for the Passover. He was crucified on the charges of practicing sorcery and leading Israel astray, in about 29 BC. This is according to the official Jewish position as published in the Talmud (Baraita Sanhedrin 43a). Jews viewed (and many still do) Christians as heretics, without hope in G-d's kingdom. Their position was so vehemently held that around AD 100, the classical rabbis pronounced a curse on Christians, which is repeated to this day in the regular Orthodox and conservative synagogue service (Shemoneh Esrei 12). Modern Jews don't at all intend this as a personal insult against Christians, but its inclusion in the Jewish prayer book is evidence of how they disdain the claim of Jesus as Messiah or Deliverer.[1] They do believe in the Old Testament promise that God would send His Messiah, but they reject Jesus as fulfilling that promise.

Islam recognizes Jesus as a prophet from Nazareth, as one born of a virgin, yet a human on the level of Adam, Noah, Abraham, and Moses. "Islam refuses the idea that Jesus was crucified on a cross, believing that Allah spared His messenger from such an ignominious death and later took him up to Himself."[2] The Koran says explicitly: "They did not kill Jesus, nor did they crucify him, but they thought they did...they knew nothing about him that was not sheer conjecture" (Koran 4:157).[3] Muslims believe that Muhammad is the final messenger, superior to all the previous prophets, and to Muslims any claim that Jesus was/ is one with Allah is very disconcerting. Again the Koran (5:74–76) strenuously refutes the divinity of Christ. To associate anything human with Allah is a grave sin, according to Islamic beliefs. Moreover, Islam teaches that humans have the capacity to choose right and wrong—to act in truth. The mere thought that a Redeemer is needed is an affront to Allah's glory. They firmly believe that the path to salvation is only attainable through the Five Pillars of Islam.

"Muslims believe that the original New Testament, which they call Injil, was the original revelation that Jesus received from Allah. They believe, however, that the Christians of today have corrupted the original Scriptures. Therefore, the Bible that is read by Christendom today is unreliable. Muslims believe that the message of Muhammad continued the original truths that were outlined in the Injil, and additionally, have corrected the errors that Christians have added."[4]

In addition to Judaism and Islam, other major religions have their own positions concerning Jesus.

Jesus' insistence that humanity's deepest need is forgiveness of sins would have struck Buddha as a deep ignorance born of the twin illusions that (A) there is a self who sins, and (B) there is a Creator who forgives. **Buddhism** is not about guilt and mercy; rather, it's about ignorance and enlightenment. According to Theravada doctrine, human beings possess everything they need to be both pure and wise. The divine doesn't even exist in the teachings of Buddha. Escape from the cycle of life is achieved through self-effort.[5] Therefore, everything that Jesus claimed is not acceptable.

Hindus see the belief about the "future kingdom of God" through their doctrine of reincarnation. They believe that humans are trapped in a circle of rebirths until they merge with Brahman. Jesus taught that every individual will face God's judgment after death, which is entirely incompatible with the Hindus fundamental understanding of the universe. Hindus look for liberation from their bodily existence into a non-bodily unity of Brahman, so Jesus' offer to become a new creation with a bodily resurrection is wholly inconsistent with Hindu beliefs. However, Hindus will include Jesus as another incarnation of one of their gods, but not that he is the singular human manifestation of any one true God. Like Buddhism, Jesus' teachings about grace are contrary to Hindus notion of human responsibility.[6]

Helen Schucman, a professor of medical psychology at Columbia University, claims that it was "Jesus" who provided her new revelation beginning in 1965, which marks the origin of **New Age** beliefs. Based on these declared revelations, she wrote *A Course in Miracles* in 1975. This course was promoted as providing everything the real Jesus told His followers to watch out for in Matthew 24—false teachers, false "Christs" who would pretend to be Jesus. While these teachings purport to instruct on these issues, New Age claims run entirely against all that Jesus taught on earth. New Age teaches there is no sin; a slain Christ has no meaning; the journey to the cross should be the last useless journey; the name of Jesus Christ as such is but a symbol to be safely used as a replacement for the many names of all the gods to which you should pray; God is in everything one can see; the recognition of God is recognition of yourself; the oneness of the Creator and the creation is your wholeness, your sanity, and your limitless power; and the Atonement is the final lesson man need learn, because it teaches that, never having sinned he has no need of salvation.[7]

However, as written earlier in this book, simply claiming a matter to be true doesn't make it so. Evidence makes confirming truth possible. The evidence for the existence of Jesus—that He was and is who He claimed to be, and that he was crucified and resurrected bodily three days later—exists beyond reasonable doubt.

Critical Proof Concerning Jesus

The Christian Bible, as a historical document, has withstood various critical proof tests, demonstrating it to be a reliable source of evidence. Let's consider some extra-biblical evidence about Jesus.

The major non-biblical source of information about Jewish happenings around the time of Jesus' lifetime comes from the writings of the Jewish historian Joseph ben Matthias, also known as Flavius Josephus. Flavius Josephus was Jewish and a general historian. He was born around AD 37–38 and died after AD 100. His education included the schools of the Sadducees, Pharisees, and the Essences, followed by three years under the tutelage of Banus. By nineteen, he attached himself to the party of the Pharisees. He later became governor of Galilee. Josephus' numerous and comprehensive writings are valuable, not only for the historical data which they contain, but also as a defense of Judaism. He writes partly as an eyewitness and partly from reports obtained from eyewitnesses; he began to make notes during the siege of Jerusalem. Both Vespasian and Titus, to whom the work was submitted, praised his accuracy. The latter even wrote on the manuscript that it ought to be published. King Agrippa II testified in no less than sixty-two letters that he found the account accurate, and similar praise was given by relatives of the king's rival, Justus of Tiberias, who wrote his history twenty years later, while Josephus described the war immediately after the events.[8]

His writings are titled *Antiquities.* Some scholars debate the writings specific to Jesus because "they are so favorable." Yet additional research proves Jesus as an historical figure who was able to perform many surprising feats, who was crucified, with specific mention of His resurrection, and that there were followers of Jesus who were still in existence at the time of the writing of *Antiquities.*[9]

Josephus mentions John the Baptist and Herod in *Antiquities,* Book 18, chapter five, paragraph two:

> Now some of the Jews thought that the destruction of Herod's army came from God, and that very justly, as a punishment of what he did against John that was called the Baptist: for Herod slew him, who was a good man, and commanded the Jews to exercise virtue, both as to righteousness towards one another, and piety towards God, and so to come to baptism; for that the washing [with water] would be acceptable to him, if they made use of it, not in order to the putting away [or the remission] of some sins [only], but for the purification of the body; supposing still that the soul was thoroughly purified beforehand by righteousness.

Josephus writes of Jesus in *Antiquities,* Book 18, chapter three, paragraph three:

> Now there was about this time Jesus, a wise man, if it be lawful to call him a man; for he was a doer of wonderful works, a teacher of such men as receive the truth with pleasure. He drew over to him both many of the Jews and many of the Gentiles. He was [the] Christ. And when Pilate, at the suggestion of the principal men amongst us, had condemned him to the cross, (9) those that loved him at the first did not forsake him, for he appeared to them alive again the third

day, (10) as the divine prophets had foretold these and ten thousand other wonderful things concerning him. And the tribe of Christians so named from him is not extinct at this day.

Josephus writes about James, the brother of Jesus in *Antiquities*, Book 20, chapter nine:

Festus was now dead, and Albinus was but upon the road; so he assembled the Sanhedrim of judges, and brought before them the brother of Jesus, who was called Christ, whose name was James, and some others [or, some of his companions]; and when he had formed an accusation against them as breakers of the law, he delivered them to be stoned: but as for those who seemed the most equitable of the citizens, and such as were the most uneasy at the breach of the laws, they disliked what was done.[10]

Tacitus was a Roman historian believed to have been born around AD 55–56 in the Roman province of Transalpine Gaul. He had a successful political course, becoming senator, consul, and eventually governor of the Roman province of Asia. He probably lived and wrote into Hadrian's reign and may have died around AD 117–120.[11] Tacitus mentions "Christus," who is **Jesus**, in Annals 15.44:

Consequently, to get rid of the report, Nero fastened the guilt and inflicted the most exquisite tortures on a class hated for their abominations, called Christians by the populace. Christus, from whom the name had its origin, suffered the extreme penalty during the reign of Tiberius at the hands of one of our procurators, Pontius Pilatus, and a most mischievous superstition, thus checked for the moment, again broke out not only in Judea, the first source of the evil, but even in Rome, where all things hideous and shameful from every part of the world find their centre and become popular.[12]

Pliny the Younger, or Gaius Plinius Caecilius Secundus (AD 62–115), was a Roman senator, nephew of Pliny the Elder, governor of Bithynia-Pontus in Asia Minor, author of a famous collection of letters.[13] Pliny wrote ten books, the tenth around AD 112, in which he wrote:

> They [the Christians] were in the habit of meeting on a certain fixed day before it was light, when they sang in alternate verses a hymn to Christ, as to a god, and bound themselves by a solemn oath, not to any wicked deeds, but never to commit any fraud, theft, or adultery, never to falsify their word, nor deny a trust when they should be called upon to deliver it up; after which, it was their custom to separate, and then reassemble to partake of food but food of an ordinary and innocent kind.[14]

Next we have the writings of the Jewish Talmud:

> On the eve of the Passover, Yeshua was hanged. For forty days before the execution took place, a herald went forth and cried, 'He is going forth to be stoned because he has practiced sorcery and enticed Israel to apostasy. Any one who can say anything in his favor let him come forward and plead on his behalf.' But since nothing was brought forward in his favor, he was hanged on the eve of the Passover![15]

Last, for the purposes of this book, is one of the writings of Lucian. Lucian lived AD 120–180 and wrote as a rhetorician, pamphleteer, and satirist in the areas of ancient Greece.[16] Lucian wrote:

> The Christians, you know, worship a man to this day the distinguished personage who introduced their novel rites, and was crucified on that account. You

see, these misguided creatures start with the general conviction that they are immortal for all time, which explains the contempt of death and voluntary self-devotion which are so common among them; and then it was impressed on them by their original lawgiver that they are all brothers, from the moment that they are converted, and deny the gods of Greece, and worship the crucified sage, and live after his laws. All this they take quite on faith, with the result that they despise all worldly goods alike, regarding them merely as common property.[17]

The above provides an extremely small sample of the extra-biblical documentation that is available in support of the events as described in the Christian New Testament concerning Jesus.

As is true of all ancient writings, none of the original texts for the Christian Bible are in existence today. What we have are copies of copies, which raises the question, "Are the documents we have today reliable copies?"

Concerning the Old Testament, the discovery of the Dead Sea Scrolls in 1947 provided the world with one of the most sensational discoveries of our age. More than one-third of the manuscripts and fragments of manuscripts are books of the Old Testament. These copies are older by at least one thousand years than the documents previously known as the oldest. This means that the Bible has stronger manuscript support than any other work of classical history—including Homer, Plato, Aristotle, Caesar, and Tacitus. Scholars who have compared the earliest existing manuscripts with manuscripts written centuries later attest that the Old Testament has remained virtually unaltered since the original writing.

In the case of the New Testament, we have exceptional evidence that what we have is effectively identical with the original documents.

The gap in time from actual events to when the events were recorded is one consideration in determining reliability. Compared to the documents of antiquity, the gap for the New Testament is relatively short. In the case of the writings of Euripides, the gap is around 1,600 years. For Plato, the gap is about 1,300 years. And Demosthenes' writings create a gap as low as 1,200 years.

More impressive is the timing of the writings of the entirety of the New Testament. Most of the twenty-seven books were written within twenty-five to thirty years of Christ's resurrection. This means that the men who wrote the accounts and letters that make up the New Testament were alive when the documents circulated, thereby open to dispute and correction from other eyewitnesses of the life, death, and resurrection of Jesus.

Numerous papyrus manuscripts have been found in Egypt in recent years, which confirm that the New Testament documents were already in existence in the first century. Sir Frederic Kenyon, a former director and principal librarian of the British Museum, wrote, "The interval then between the dates of original composition and the earliest extant [existing] evidence becomes so small as to be in fact negligible, and the last foundation for any doubt that the Scriptures have come down to us substantively as they were written had now been removed. Both the authenticity and the general integrity of the books of the New Testament may be regarded as finally established."[18]

The Bible has more objective, verifiable evidence in support that it has not been substantively altered or amended, which is a claim that no other faith can make regarding their document(s) of religious authority. This reality is an anchor to my faith!

Chapter Fourteen

The Biblical and Historical Birth of Jesus

For most, the extra-biblical information presented in the previous chapter should provide enough evidence to allow us to now seriously consider Jesus from the historical biblical perspective. As we do, we need to keep in mind the Christian understanding of God as three Persons in one, explained in chapter ten. God is God the Father, or Creator; God the Son, or Redeemer; and God the Holy Spirit, or Power—also referred to as the Trinity.

It is also important to know that Old Testament Scriptures were written as many as 1,450 years before the birth of Jesus. To provide a frame of reference, it is good to understand the dates of the writings of its various books. The collection of Scriptures known as Psalms is estimated to have been written 1400–450 BC. The book of Isaiah, written by a man regarded as the greatest Old Testament Prophet, is believed to have been written in the years 700–681 BC. The book of Genesis is commonly accepted to have been written by Moses likely between 1450 and 1410 BC.

The Human Lineage of Jesus

In Genesis, God declared that He would provide a Deliverer, to redeem His creation from the ravages of sin. Using the Bible along with extra-biblical evidence, we can historically follow the lineage of the first man Adam, and the first woman Eve to the offspring of Noah, Abraham, Isaac, Jacob, Judah, King David, all the way to a young virgin woman named Mary.[1] Mary was the one chosen by God to bear the Seed promised in Genesis 3—the Deliverer/Redeemer.

Specific Conditions for Jesus' Existence

According to the Bible prophecies, there were three requirements that Jesus had to meet to be the Promised Deliverer. First, He had to be a *male*, born of a woman as first predicted in Genesis 3:15—specifically, a virgin woman, according to Isaiah 7:14. He had to become one of us humans to redeem us. No angel could have borne our sin; He had to represent us in all our human respects.

Second, He had to be *sinless* in order to have the perfection God demands. As sinners, we cannot pay for our own sin, even if we suffered forever, much less could we pay for the sin of someone else. The acceptance of the sacrifice depended on its value, and its perfection. Moreover, with all of humanity inheriting this sinful condition from birth, mankind needed someone greater than us, able to satisfy the debt of sin. Redemption cannot occur when one sinful human dies for another sinful human.

Third, He also had to be of *God*, so that it could be said that God personally undertook a rescue mission to reconcile sinful humanity unto Himself. If salvation is of the Lord, He had to provide the very sacrifice He demanded.[2] So with God as His Father, Jesus was the Son of God—as part of the Trinity, He was God Himself. It was prophesied in Psalm 2:7–8, accordingly:

> The king proclaims the Lord's decree: "The Lord
> said to me, 'You are my Son. Today, I have become
> your Father. Only ask, and I will give you the nations
> as your inheritance, the ends of the earth as your
> possession.'" (NLT)

Jesus' Earthly Conception

The biblical account explains that the angel Gabriel appeared to Mary, while she was engaged to be married to Joseph (who could also trace his lineage to King David). Gabriel revealed that she had found great favor with God and she would be the one to conceive a Son who was to be called Jesus. Gabriel explained this Son would be of the Highest, and the Lord God will give Him the throne of His father David, "And He will reign over the house of Jacob forever, and of His kingdom there will be no end." This perplexed Mary because she was a virgin, so she inquired of Gabriel. Gabriel replied that God's Holy Spirit would overshadow her and her Son therefore will be called the Son of God.[3]

At the right time, the Holy Spirit overshadowed Mary and miraculously the human egg from her womb and the divine counterpart were joined. Mary conceived a baby that was both fully human and fully God, making this baby essentially the same as all human beings, yet very, very different.

Notice how Jesus' conception satisfies the specific conditions for His existence. To understand why the conditions were essential, let's review. When Adam, as the mortal father of all humanity, sinned, the whole human race that would descend from him was impacted. In order for God to personally pay the debt of sin in our behalf in the person of Jesus, Jesus could not have a human father or else he'd be the same as every other human being and He could not live in His deity. In order to be a true substitute sacrifice for humanity, He had to completely live as a human. Scriptures reveal that Jesus willingly laid down His deity and lived in humanity, being tempted in every way common to man, yet He did not sin.[4] He refused to operate in His deity while on earth. Jesus laid down His deity. He did not give it up.

Almighty God, in the second person of the Trinity, motivated by tremendous love and mercy, humbled Himself and took on the form of humanity so that He could provide a way for God's creation to be restored unto Him.

Birthplace of Jesus

The Bible records that shortly before Jesus was born, Mary and Joseph traveled to return to their town of origin, due to a census required by the Roman government. They left Nazareth and traveled to their home town of Bethlehem in the northeast area of Galilee. Because of the many others also returning to their home town, the inns were overcrowded. Mary was ready to give birth, and so Mary and Joseph took refuge in a stable. It was a manger where animals are kept that served as the humble place of birth for Jesus, Almighty God in human form.

I find it interesting that King David, who had ruled over Israel about one thousand years before, was also born in Bethlehem. And Rachel, the beloved wife of Jacob, one of the Jewish/Christian patriarchs, was buried in Bethlehem. Even more noteworthy is the prophet Micah, who lived about seven hundred years before Jesus' birth, proclaimed that Bethlehem would be the birthplace for the Messiah.[5]

Historically we know that Jesus was born around 4 BC, perhaps as late as 8 BC. Scripturally, we read that about this same time, *wise men*—astronomers—from the East traveled under the guidance of a star. They believed this miraculous star indicated that a new and wonderful King had just been born. So they stopped in Jerusalem to inquire of Herod, the Roman king of the Jews. They had calculated the estimated date of the birth of the Messiah and believed the great star to be evidence of the Messiah's birth.

History provides evidence of the existence of one or more unusual "stars" appearing around the time of Jesus' birth. Modern scholars speculate about the star as a potential meteor, or an alignment of celestial bodies, or a literal star, without ruling out the prospect of a supernatural phenomenon. Noteworthy is that ancient Chinese astronomers record, a star-like object hovering somewhere over the Middle East for several days in the year 5 BC. Other astronomers speculate plausible alternative cosmic prospects based on known reoccurring events in the skies, events that were unique to the time of Jesus' birth.[6]

The Bible records that while Mary and Joseph were in Bethlehem, shepherds were watching their flocks by night. Scriptures indicate that an angel of the Lord appeared to the shepherds, and the glory of the Lord shone around them. They were greatly afraid, but the angel spoke saying, "Do not be afraid, for behold I bring you tidings of great joy which will be to all people. For there is born to you this day, in the city of David, a Savior, who is Christ the Lord. And this will be the sign to you: You will find a Babe wrapped in swaddling cloths, lying in a manger. And suddenly, there was with the angel a multitude of the heavenly host praising God and saying: 'Glory to God in the highest, and on earth peace, goodwill toward men!'"(Luke 2:10–14). The shepherds went with haste to find Mary, Joseph, and the Babe, and they found them just as the angel proclaimed. While there, the shepherds told all of their angelic experience, marveling at the birth of the Messiah, glorifying and praising God for all the things they had heard, seen, and been told.[7] Mary marveled too, but scriptures reveal she pondered it all in her heart. Could the star the wise men saw and the heavenly host the shepherds saw be two experiences of the phenomenon that ancient Chinese astronomers record?

The Timing of Jesus' Arrival

There is a very specific prophecy recorded in Daniel 9:25 abut the time when the Messiah would come. This is among the most amazing concerning the precise time of His arrival in Jerusalem. Britt Gillette, author and avid student of Bible prophecy, has a truly compelling website, BrittGillette.com,[8] where he beautifully unfolds Old Testament prophecy tied to the New Testament fulfillment, some of which is detailed below.

Daniel 9:25–26 records that the angel Gabriel appeared to Daniel and told him the exact number of days that will pass between the time the command is given to rebuild Jerusalem and the time the Messiah will appear in Jerusalem. "Now listen and understand! Seven sets of seven plus sixty-two sets of seven will pass from the time the command is given to rebuild Jerusalem: until a ruler—the Anointed One—comes. Jerusalem will be rebuilt with streets and strong defenses, despite the perilous times. After this period of sixty-two sets of seven, the Anointed One will be killed, appearing to have accomplished nothing, and a ruler will arise whose armies will destroy the city and the Temple. The end will come with a flood, and war and its miseries are decreed from that time to the very end" (NLT).

Gillette explains that only one historical person's life fulfills this prophecy of the Messiah—Jesus of Nazareth: according to the Book of Daniel, 483 years [(7 × 7) + (62 × 7)] would pass between the time the command is given to rebuild Jerusalem until the Anointed One would come. Since a biblical year is 360 days, we're actually being told that 173,880 days will pass. So to find out if this prophecy was fulfilled, we only need to count forward 173,880 days from the time of the command and see if anyone entered Jerusalem and was killed, appearing to have accomplished nothing. If such a person existed, the Word of God confirms that person was the Messiah.

Pamela Christian

So when was the command given? The book of Nehemiah 2:1–8 tells us. The command to rebuild Jerusalem was given in the twentieth year of the reign of Artaxerxes (446 BC) during the month of Nisan (March/April).

Using the Calendar Conversion Tool,[9] we can calculate the time frame in which the prophecy must be fulfilled. Counting 173,880 days into the future from Nissan 1 to Nissan 30 in the year 446 BC (the year 3315 in the Jewish calendar), we learn that the prophecy must be fulfilled between the dates of 13 April AD 31 and 12 May AD 31.

Gregorian calendar: 20 March 446 BC or Jewish calendar: 1 Nisan 3315 plus 173,880 days (360 days × 483 years) comes to 13 April AD 31 on the Gregorian calendar and 4 Iyyar 3791 on the Jewish calendar.

Also, Gregorian calendar: 18 April 446 BC or Jewish calendar: 30 Abib/Nisan 3315 plus 173,880 days (360 days × 483 years) comes to 12 May AD 31 on the Gregorian calendar and 4 Sivan 3791 on the Jewish calendar.

Did anyone appear in Jerusalem between 13 April AD 31 and 12 May AD 31 who fulfilled the prophecies of the Messiah and was killed, "appearing to accomplish nothing"? Yes: Jesus of Nazareth. During the Passover festivities in Jerusalem in the year AD 31, Jesus was killed this way. According to Dr. David Reagan's (Bible scholar and founder/director of Lion and Lamb Ministries) commentary on the subject, the New Testament provides evidence that two Sabbaths occurred, one on Thursday and one on Saturday, during the week of Jesus of Nazareth's crucifixion. Given other historical records and evidence, we can be certain that the crucifixion of Jesus occurred on the twenty-fourth of April AD 31, a date that falls between the predetermined time frame of 13 April to 12 May for the Messiah's appearance.[10]

Because of this information, we can be certain that Jesus of Nazareth fulfilled the requirements of this messianic prophecy. Jesus fulfilled all forty-four messianic Old Testament prophecies concerning the Savior's first coming. No other historical individual appeared during April or May of AD 31 who could fulfill this prophecy.[11] Even if anyone else could have fulfilled all the other prophesies concerning the Messiah, the specific timing of His coming is tremendously significant.

Chapter Fifteen

Prophecies Fulfilled Concerning Jesus

Prophecy is the foretelling of an event. Only if the prediction comes to pass is it a true prophecy. Anything else is a lie. Experts estimate that there are over three hundred prophecies concerning Jesus *alone* that have been fulfilled. In keeping with the definition of faith, I believe there is more than sufficient—in fact, I believe there is overwhelming objective, verifiable evidence that has come to pass to allow me to believe by faith for what is predicted and yet to be fulfilled. This to me is exceedingly exciting!

In the last chapter, I provided information about the biblical and historical evidence regarding the birth of Jesus. In this chapter, I want to share some prophecies concerning the life of Jesus. There is so much prophecy in support of Jesus being the promised Redeemer—the promised Messiah. The astounding number and detailed fulfillment of prophecy is one major body of evidence to convince us that He was and is who He claimed to be.

The Significance of Testimony

In the process of discovering truth, it is logical and reasonable to seek sufficient confirmation. Using the legal system as an example, when the truth about a defendant is needed, the testimony of eyewitnesses or personal witnesses is of great value. However, the acceptance of any claim made by a witness is based on the witness's background, reputation, and testimony. The character and reliability of the witness are very important. Any witness who has been known to lie is far less likely to be trusted, even if he's telling the truth in the moment.

Of all the people God planned to walk the face of this earth, His Son Jesus would be the most outlandish. To help people believe the truth about Jesus, God planned a forerunner—a *witness*—to testify in advance about the Messiah, the Christ. To further help people, God prophesied through Isaiah, one of the greatest Old Testament patriarchs, that such a witness would precede the coming of the Messiah. This is recorded in Isaiah 40:3–5: "The voice of one crying out in the wilderness: 'Prepare the way of the Lord; make straight in the desert a highway for our God. Every valley shall be exalted and every mountain and hill brought low; the crooked places shall be made straight and the rough places smooth; the glory of the Lord shall be revealed, and all flesh shall see it together; for the mouth of the Lord has spoken.'"

Another place where this witness is and the coming of the Messiah are predicted is in Malachi 3:1: "Behold, I send My messenger and he will prepare the way before Me. And the Lord whom you seek will suddenly come to His temple, even the Messenger of the covenant, in whom you delight. Behold, He is coming says the Lord of Hosts." Malachi 4:5–6 reads, "Behold, I will send you Elijah the prophet before the coming of the great and dreadful day of the Lord. And he will turn the hearts of the fathers to the children, and the hearts of the children to their fathers, lest I come and strike the earth with a curse."

As is proven in the New Testament era, John the Baptist is the forerunner these Old Testament scriptures proclaim. His role was to provide advance testimony to prepare the people to believe in and receive Jesus as the Promised One. As you will read, the life and character of John the Baptist was without reproach, making him a most suitable witness concerning Jesus.

The Angelic Proclamation about the Forerunner

Prior to the angel Gabriel appearing to Mary, as noted in the previous chapter, he appeared to Mary's relative Zacharias. He and his wife Elizabeth had been barren and prayed to God to conceive. The angel Gabriel proclaimed that their prayers were heard and Elizabeth would conceive a boy child that they were to name John. Gabriel foretold that they would have joy and gladness and many will rejoice at their son's birth, "for he will be great in the sight of the Lord, and shall drink neither wine nor strong drink. He will also be filled with the Holy Spirit even from his mother's womb. John, Gabriel declared, would turn many of the children of Israel to the Lord their God. He will also go before Him in the spirit and power of Elijah, 'to turn their hearts of the fathers to the children' and the disobedient to the wisdom of the just, to make ready a people prepared for the Lord" (Luke 1:5–17).

The Early Life of Jesus

We know little about the life of Jesus as He grew to be an adult. Matthew 2 and Luke 2 provide some information. We know as He grew he increased in wisdom and in stature and in favor with God and man. Scriptures reveal that Mary and Joseph had other children after Him. We know that He followed in His earthly father's trade of carpentry. Matthew and Luke 1 reveal that Jesus had a cousin, just a few months older than He. His life and ministry was also miraculously revealed by God. John the Baptist was Jesus' cousin, on Mary's side, who was born about six months earlier than Jesus.

The Ministry of John the Baptist

As an adult, John traveled about the wilderness of Judea, around the river Jordan. A word from the Lord came to him to proclaim to the people. He came preaching saying, "Repent, for all the kingdom of heaven is at hand." He cried out to the people to seek baptism and to repent for the remission or lessening of their sins. John, who became known as John the Baptist, proclaimed the coming of the Messiah, baptizing the people in preparation to receive Him.

Much of the preaching and heralding of John the Baptist is contained in Matthew 3:5–17, Luke 3:1–20, and John 1:19–28. These report that multitudes of people heeded his message and prepared themselves for the Messiah. John accused the Jewish religious leaders of the day for misleading the people and serving their personal gain. In Luke 3:16, we read the words of John: "I indeed baptize you with water; but One mightier than I is coming, whose sandal strap am not worthy to loose. He will baptize you with the Holy Spirit and fire." John was also prophesying what the faithful would soon experience after Jesus' death, as recorded in Acts 2 concerning the baptism of the Holy Spirit.

The Beginning of Jesus' Ministry

When Jesus was about thirty years of age, He came to John the Baptist at the River Jordan seeking to be baptized. John saw Jesus coming and declared, "Behold! The Lamb of God who takes away the sin of the world! This is He of whom I said, 'After me comes a Man who is preferred before me, for He was before me. I did not know Him; but that He should be revealed to Israel, therefore, I came baptizing with water.'"[1]

As Jesus approached wanting to be baptized, John tried to prevent this, declaring that Jesus should be baptizing him! However, Jesus persuaded John, explaining that it was necessary for Jesus to fulfill all that God required. With that, John agreed. John submerged Jesus, and when Jesus came up from the water, scriptures reveal that the heavens were opened up to Him and He saw the Spirit of God descending like a dove and alighting upon Him: "And suddenly a voice came from heaven, saying, "This is My beloved Son, in whom I am well pleased."[2] John the Baptist bore witness and testimony of this amazing occurrence. This act of Jesus' baptism is yet another prophetic fulfillment, specifically as written in Isaiah 11:2: "And the Spirit of the Lord will rest on Him—the Spirit of wisdom and understanding, the Spirit of counsel and might, the Spirit of knowledge and fear of the Lord" (NLT).

The New Testament, along with extra-biblical evidence, has much to say about the life and ministry of Jesus. Simply reading through John's Gospel, you can learn a great deal about Him. Jesus clearly claimed to be King of the Jews—to be the long-awaited Messiah. He went about teaching and preaching and performing many miracles. He made the blind see. He healed others of sickness and disease. He even raised some from the dead. These works were also foretold in Isaiah 35:5–6.

His popularity grew among the people, to the dissatisfaction of the Jewish leaders known as the Pharisees and the Sadducees. Moreover, Jesus' claims to forgive sin, which the Jewish leaders rightly believed only God could do, infuriated them. They did not believe Jesus was the Messiah, and the Son of God, and their anger grew so intense that they plotted to kill Him.

Prophecies Concerning the Popularity of Jesus

Malachi 3:1 predicted that Jesus would enter the Temple with authority. Matthew 21:12–13 clearly reveals that He acted with this authority by driving out the corrupt money changers, defending God's Temple, which is to be a house of prayer, not a den of thieves.

Isaiah 61:1–2 declares that the Messiah would preach the good news to the poor, comfort the brokenhearted, and announce the year of the Lord's favor. This was fulfilled as recorded in Luke 4:16–21.

Psalm 35:19 prophesied that the Messiah would be hated without a cause. The people's unwarranted hatred is recorded throughout the Gospel books of the New Testament.

The Old Testament predicted that the Messiah would enter Jerusalem riding on a donkey (**Zechariah 9:9**). And indeed this too happened, as recorded in Matthew 21:1–4. Jesus uniquely fulfilled all the Old Testament prophecies concerning the Messiah, the Deliverer, the Redeemer, the Savior of all who will believe by faith. He arrived at the appointed time riding on a donkey, as predicted hundreds of years before.

Prophecies Concerning the Rejection of Jesus

- **Isaiah 53:3** prophesied that the Messiah would be rejected. John 18–19 documents this rejection by describing an exceedingly disturbing series of events where Jesus was betrayed, wrongly accused, illegally tried, ridiculed, scourged, brutally beaten, then crucified because of the hatred of the Jewish leaders. Jewish accusations brought the sentence of death; Roman execution completed the sentence. Together, they represented the religious authority and world government of the day.

- **Isaiah 53:7** predicted that the Messiah would be silent in front of His accusers. Matthew 26:62–63 documents that when he was wrongly and illegally tried and accused, Jesus remained silent.

- **Psalm 118:22** declared that Jesus will be rejected by the unbelieving Jews. First Peter 2:4–8 confirmed the occurrence of this rejection in verse 4, which states, "Coming to Him as to a living stone rejected indeed by men, but chosen by God and precious."

- **Psalm 41:9** predicted that Jesus would be betrayed by a friend. John 13:18–19 and John 13:26–27 tells of one of Jesus' disciples who'd been with Him for nearly three years, witnessed all the good Jesus did and taught, then betrayed Him. Judas turned Jesus over to the Jewish leadership, whose intent was to kill Him.

- This act of betrayal is even more detailed in **Zechariah 11:12**, which prophesied that Jesus' betrayer would agree to his deed in exchange for thirty pieces of silver. Matthew 26:14–15 confirms this happened. **Zechariah 11:13** predicted that the thirty pieces of silver would be thrown to the potters in the Temple of the Lord. Matthew 27:3–8 confirms that when Judas learned Jesus was condemned to die, he was filled with remorse, returned to the Temple, and threw the pieces of silver on the floor at the priests and leaders. Then Judas went up and hanged himself. The leaders picked up the money and considered their law, which states that money used for murder couldn't be put into the Temple treasury, so they decided to buy the potter's field next to the Temple to be a cemetery for foreigners.

- These unbelieving Jewish leaders who were supposed to know their own Scriptures didn't recognize the Messiah, neither did they consider their plot to murder Jesus inconsistent with their own laws. However, they knew the laws concerning blood money. Without realizing it, they fulfilled Old Testament prophecy, further establishing that the very One they rejected as Messiah was in fact who He claimed to be, the Messiah.

Prophecies Concerning the Death of Jesus

There are several Old Testament prophecies that predict specific events concerning Jesus' death that New Testament scriptures confirm happened. What follows are some of my favorites:

- **Psalm 34:19–20** declares that the Messiah's bones would not be broken. **Psalm 22:14** prophesies that His life will be poured out like water. John 19:31–34 reports that these two were fulfilled in detail on the day of Jesus' crucifixion.

- **Zachariah 13:7** predicts that the Messiah would be struck down and His disciples scattered. In Matthew 26:31, Jesus Himself predicted that all His disciples would betray Him. Matthew 26:56 records that later this indeed happened, as all His disciples deserted Him and fled.

- **Deuteronomy 21:22–23** expresses that God cursed any man executed for breaking one of God's commands. His body hanging on a pole was a public display of judgment. Jesus took on this curse, for all mankind for all time, when He died on the cross, as confirmed with 1 Peter 2:24. The Apostle Paul reiterates this in Galatians 3:13–14: "Christ has redeemed us from the curse of the law, having become a curse for us (for it is written, 'Cursed is everyone who hangs on a tree'), that the blessings of Abraham might come upon the Gentiles in Christ Jesus, that we might receive the promise of the Spirit through faith."

- **Deuteronomy 21:23** also commanded that the offender's body not be left on the pole overnight. As we know from

177

the Gospels, Jesus' body was taken down and placed into the tomb before nightfall. This is according to Matthew 27:57–60 and Mark 15:42–46.

- **Isaiah 53:9** foretold that the Messiah would be buried like a criminal and placed in a rich man's grave. This occurred when His body was placed in the new tomb owned by Joseph of Arimathea, as recorded in Matthew 27:59–60.

- Jesus spoke many times concerning the details surrounding His death. In one instance, when challenged by the unbelieving scribes and Pharisees, because He knew their hearts, He responded, "An evil and adulterous generation seeks after a sign, and no sign shall be given to it except the sign of the prophet Jonah. For as Jonah was three days and three nights in the belly of the great fish, so will the Son of Man be three days and three nights in the heart of the earth."[3]

- The purpose in the Messiah's death was clarified in **Isaiah 53:4**: "Yet it was our weaknesses He carried; it was our sorrows that weighed Him down. And we thought His troubles were a punishment from God for His own sins! But he was wounded and crushed for our sins. He was beaten that we might have peace. He was whipped, and we were healed! All of us have strayed away like sheep. We have left God's paths to follow our own. Yet the Lord laid on Him the guilt of sins of us all." Verse 8: "From prison and trial they led Him away to His death. But who among the people realized that He was dying for their sins–that He was suffering their punishment?" Verses 10–12: "But it was the Lord's good plan to crush him and fill Him with grief. Yet when His life is made an offering for sin, He will have a multitude of children, many heirs. He will enjoy a long life, and the Lord's plan will prosper in His hands. When He sees all that is accomplished by His anguish, He will be satisfied. And because of what He has experienced, my righteous servant will make it possible for many to be counted righteous, for He will bear all their sins. I will give Him the honors of One who is mighty and great, because He exposed Himself to death. He was counted among those who were sinners. He bore the sins of many and interceded for sinners." This prophecy was fulfilled in the crucifixion of Jesus, and the Apostle Paul made it clear in Romans 3:23–26: "For everyone has sinned; we all fall short of God's glorious standard. Yet God, with undeserved kindness, declares that we are righteous. He did this through Christ Jesus when he freed us from the penalty for our sins. For God presented Jesus as the sacrifice for sin. People are made right with God when they believe that Jesus sacrificed his life, shedding his blood. This sacrifice shows that God was being fair when he held back and did not punish those who sinned in times past, for he was looking ahead and including them in what he would do in this present time. God did this to demonstrate his righteousness, for he himself is fair and just, and he declares sinners to be right in his sight when they believe in Jesus" (NLT).

Prophecies Concerning the Crucifixion of Jesus

• The people were greatly stirred up with all that took place in Jerusalem that night. Consider the multitudes who had earnestly followed Him before, in contrast to the anger and riotous atmosphere that ensued literally overnight. Jesus was taken before the Jewish government, the Sanhedrin, then before Pontius Pilate, then Herod, and back to Pontius Pilate. Clearly a bloodthirsty mob had been incited. At the insistence of the Jewish chief priests, rulers, and the people, Pontius Pilate reluctantly granted what the people wanted, though he himself did not believe Jesus was guilty.[4]

- **Psalm 35:11** predicted that the Messiah would be accused by false witnesses. Mark 14:56 confirms this happened. The long night of illegal trial and public ridicule and utterly brutal, barbaric treatment ultimately resulted in Jesus being wrongly sentenced to death by way of crucifixion.

- **Psalm 22** in its entirety is a prophetic perspective of Jesus as He hung on the cross. **Psalm 22:14–16** speaks of His death with His hands and feet pierced. The practice of crucifixion was not known at the time this scripture passage was written. The Romans introduced crucifixion hundreds, some say as many as one thousand years, afterward.

- **Isaiah 50:6** predicted that the Messiah would be beaten, mocked and spit upon. **Isaiah 52:13–14** states He would be beaten, bloodied, and disfigured. Matthew 26:67 and John 19:1–3 confirm that Jesus was treated in this manner.

- **Psalm 22:7–8** declared that the Messiah would be mocked and told to save Himself. Psalm 22:16 prophesied that His enemies would pierce His hands and feet. Psalm 69:21 predicted the Messiah would be given vinegar and gall to drink. Matthew 27:41–44, John 19:17–18, and Mark 15:23 confirm that each of these acts occurred.

- **Psalm 22:17–18** predicted that the Messiah's garments would be sought by his enemies and that they would cast lots.

John 19:23–14 details this event, which occurred as they were preparing to crucify Him.

• Mark 15 describes the events leading up to Jesus' crucifixion, with verse 25 revealing it took place in the third hour of the day. Some time during nine to ten a.m., they crucified Him. Verse 33 reveals that when the sixth hour came, which is noon to one p.m., a darkness covered the whole land until the ninth hour, which is three to four p.m. While He hung on the cross, beaten and tortured, ridiculed and scorned, with the weight of all the sins of the whole world on Him, in the ninth hour, Jesus cried out in a loud voice, "My God! My God! Why have You forsaken Me?" Psalm 22, penned by King David as much as one thousand years before, foretells the anguish the Messiah would endure, so great it would seem that He'd been forsaken by the Father. Then shortly thereafter, Jesus cried out with a loud voice again and breathed His last (Matthew 15:37).

• At the very moment of Jesus' death, Matthew 15:38 reveals that the veil of the Temple where the Jews worshiped was torn from top to bottom. This veil was not a thin lacy veil such as a bride wears. This veil was four inches thick and measured sixty feet high and thirty feet wide according to Matthew 27:51, Mark 15:38, and Luke 23:45. Considering the manner in which the veil was hung, its enormous size and weight, and that traditional Jewish literature indicates it took three hundred priests to handle it,[4] it's improbable that man could tear it from bottom to top. A tear from top to bottom implies that God, not man, tore the veil.[5]

• Hebrews 9:1–9 tells us that in the Temple, a veil separated the Holy of Holies, the earthly dwelling place of God's presence, from the rest of the Temple where people worshipped. This signified that man was separated from God by sin (**Isaiah 59:1–2**). Only the high priest was permitted to pass beyond this veil. He did so once each year (Exodus 30:10; Hebrews 9:7) to enter into God's presence for all of Israel and to make atonement for their sins (Leviticus 16).

- The Psalmist was given prophetic insight about Jesus' ascension to heaven, "When You ascended to the heights, You led a crowd of captives" (**Psalm 68:18**). The faithful who had believed God for His promise of a Deliverer, who died before Jesus appeared, were released from their place of waiting (which the Bible calls Paradise) when Jesus ascended and were taken to heaven with Him as the Apostle Paul wrote in Ephesians 4:8.

The New Covenant

By Jesus' death, the entrance into the Holy of Holies was open for all people, for all time, both Jew and Gentile. When the veil was torn, God moved out of that place never again to dwell in a temple made with hands (Acts 17:24). God's purposes for that Temple and its religious system were left desolate. Later, in AD 70, the Temple was destroyed, which fulfilled Jesus' prophesy recorded in Luke 13:35. As long as the temple stood, it signified the continuation of the Old Covenant. Hebrews 9:8–9 refers to the age that was passing away as the New Covenant was being established (Hebrews 8:13). Above all, the tearing of the veil at the moment of Jesus' death dramatically symbolized that His sacrifice, the shedding of His own blood, was a sufficient and complete atonement for sin.

Now Christ has become and is viewed as the superior High Priest, and believers in His finished work partake of His better priesthood.

Believers can now enter the Holy of Holies through Him. Hebrews 10:19–20 says that the faithful enter into the sanctuary by the "blood of Jesus, by the new and living way which He opened for us through the veil, that is, through His flesh." This passage reveals that as Jesus' flesh was torn, He tore the veil that then allowed for direct access to God through belief in the High Priest, Jesus.

The tearing of Christ's flesh and the tearing of the Temple veil are quite significant, as explained in glorious detail in the book of Hebrews. The things of the Temple were shadows of things to come, and they all point to Jesus Christ. He was the veil to the Holy of Holies, and through His death, anyone who believes and receives Jesus by faith now has free access to God.[6]

This chapter is not intended to provide an exhaustive list of all the fulfilled prophecies concerning Jesus. However, it is my hope that you've read enough to be in awe, as I've come to believe and experience Jesus is who He claimed to be.

Chapter Sixteen

Evidence for the Resurrection of Jesus

The New Testament, as supported by extra-biblical evidence considered previously in this book, provides eyewitness accounts of those who saw Jesus on earth after His confirmed death on the Cross. There were over five hundred eyewitnesses who boldly declared their experience, which was documented during the lifetime of the eyewitnesses. Had their testimonies been documented after their lifetime there would be reason for suspicion. The fact that they personally and publicly testified of their experiences gives evidence that they were utterly confident of their claims.

Just as we experience today, no two people see or comprehend the same events in exactly the same way. Ask any police officer who has ever interviewed eyewitnesses about the happenings of an automobile accident, and he'll tell you that each person reports the events a bit differently. The key to finding the truth is to overlay the testimonies and find that which is consistent.

The four Gospel books of the New Testament were written by four different men who were eyewitnesses to the life, death, and resurrection of Jesus Christ. They each recall details a little differently. So here in this chapter I've attempted to provide you a reasonable compilation of the events surrounding the days following Jesus' death.

The Tomb of Jesus

John 20:1 reveals: "On the first day of the week, Mary Magdalene went early to the tomb while it was still dark and saw that the stone [that sealed the tomb shut] had been taken from the tomb." Luke 24:10 lists more about this: "Joanna and Mary, the mother of James, and other women were with her." Luke 24:1 explains they had various spices with them to embalm the body. This occurred three days after Jesus' crucifixion.

Matthew 28:2 reports that there was a great earthquake: "For an angel of the Lord descended from heaven, and came and rolled back the stone from the door, and sat on it." The Roman guards who were stationed there to make certain the body was not removed shook for fear of the angel and fell down as if they were dead.

John 20:1–18 reveals that when the women first arrived, they saw that the stone had been rolled away from the tomb. Peering in and seeing that the body of Jesus was gone, they feared that His body had been stolen. Weeping, Mary Magdalene saw two angels—one sitting where Jesus' head would have been, the other where His feet would have been. Luke 24:5–7 records one of the angels asking, "Why do you seek the living among the dead? He is not here, but is risen! Remember how He spoke to you when He was still in Galilee, saying, 'The Son of Man must be delivered into the hands of sinful men, and be crucified, and the third day rise again.'" Matthew 28:5 indicates that the angel also said, "Do not be afraid, for I know that you seek Jesus who was crucified. He is not here; for he is risen, as He said. Come, see the place where the Lord lay." Luke 20:11 includes the angels asking Mary, "Woman, why are you weeping?" She replied, "Because they have taken away my Lord and I do not know where they have laid Him."

Matthew 28:7–9 reveals that the angels instructed the women to "Go quickly and tell Jesus' disciples that He is risen from the dead, and indeed, He is going before you into Galilee; there you will see Him. Behold, I have told you." The women were on their way to tell the disciples what the angles proclaimed when Jesus Himself met them.

When Mary Magdalene turned around, she saw a man standing there. He asked her, "Woman, why are you weeping? Whom are you seeking?" Supposing Him to be the gardener, she answered, "Sir, if You have carried Him away, tell me where You have laid Him, and I will take Him away." He simply called her name, "Mary!" And with that, she recognized He was Jesus (John 20:14–18). Matthew 28:9 includes that Jesus encouraged them, "Rejoice!" and the women fell down to worship Him at His feet. The Apostle John reports in John 20:17 that Jesus responded, "Do not cling to Me, for I have not yet ascended to My Father; but go to My brethren and say to them, 'I am ascending to My Father and your Father, and to My God and your God.'" Matthew 28:10 adds Jesus instructing the women, "Do not be afraid. Go and tell My brethren to go to Galilee, and there they will see Me."

So they ran quickly with joy to tell the disciples that Jesus' tomb was *empty*! Luke 24:9 continues: "They returned from the tomb and told all these things to the eleven and to all the rest." Their words seemed like idle tales and no one believed the women. But with a chance it could be true, according to John 20:2–11, upon hearing what the women reported, Peter and John ran to see for themselves. When they arrived one at a time, the two men entered the tomb and saw that the linen cloths that were used to wrap the body were lying there with the handkerchief that had been around Jesus' head neatly folded and placed separate from the linen clothes. Peter and John knew the Old Testament scripture stated that the Messiah must rise from the dead. They knew the scriptures, but didn't understand them fully. Clearly, they failed to remember what Jesus had personally said about His own resurrection. With all that they had witnessed, Peter and John went away to their own homes, no doubt in deep wonderment.

The Forty Days Following Jesus' Death

Many people in the New Testament period were eyewitnesses to the nearly risen Messiah. In addition to the appearances noted above, He appeared to two of His disciples the day of the resurrection, on the road to Emmaus. He walked with them, conversed with them, and even further explained why he had to suffer as He did from the scriptures. As evening approached, He went into their home to dine with them. And when He took the bread, broke it, and gave it to them, only then did Cleopas and Simon realize it was Jesus, and immediately He vanished (Luke 24:13–35).

Next, He appeared to the ten disciples, Thomas not among them, at Jerusalem on the evening of the Resurrection Day. While they were gathered in a room with the doors shut, Jesus suddenly appeared. The apostles were terrified and Jesus bid them peace. He knew their thoughts and asked, "Why are you troubled? And why do doubts arise in your hearts? Behold My hands and My feet, that it is I, Myself. Handle Me and see for a spirit does not have flesh and bones as you see I have." They still did not believe, so He asked, "Do you have any food here?" They gave Him a piece of broiled fish and honey, and He ate, clearly to prove that He was not a spirit, but was present with a newly resurrected body.

Jesus then said, "These are the words which I spoke to you while I was still with you, that all things must be fulfilled which were written in the Law of Moses and the Prophets and the Psalms concerning Me." And He opened their understanding so they could comprehend the scriptures. Then speaking to them again, He said, "Thus it is written, and thus it was necessary for the Christ to suffer and rise from the dead the third day, and that repentance and remission of sins should be preached in His name to all nations, beginning at Jerusalem. And you are witnesses of these things. Behold, I send you the Promise of My Father upon you; but tarry in the city of Jerusalem until you are endued with power from high." This is recorded in John 20:19–23 and Luke 24:36–49.

Some eight days later, when all the apostles were gathered, again Jesus appeared, this time it seems for Thomas, as recorded in John 20:26. He was not previously with the apostles when Jesus appeared to them, and he doubted their report. So Jesus returned so that Thomas may see for himself and believe.

We read in John 21:1–23 that the disciples later went fishing at the Sea of Galilee when Jesus appeared on the beach waiting for them. This was the third time He appeared to them, and this time, He ate breakfast with them. He also restored Peter, who, as Jesus had predicted, denied Him three times.

Matthew 28:16–20 records the eleven disciples going to the mountain in Galilee as Jesus had instructed them. There He appeared again. Here Jesus spoke the following words: "All authority has been given to Me in heaven and on earth. Go therefore and make disciples of all the nations, baptizing them in the name of the Father and of the Son and of the Holy Spirit, teaching them to observe all things that I have commanded you; and lo, I am with you always, even to the end of the age."

In addition to all this, the Apostle Paul provides a list of times the Messiah appeared after his death. First Corinthians 15:6 indicates that Jesus was once seen by over five hundred brethren *at the same* time. Note that the majority of these people were still alive at the time he wrote the letter to the Corinthian believers. This is significant because what the Apostle Paul claimed could be confirmed as true by the eyewitnesses. In 1 Corinthians 15:7, Paul writes that Jesus also appeared to James, though no details are provided.

The Ascension of Jesus

Immediately before His final Ascension—returning bodily to heaven— the Apostles accompanied Jesus from Jerusalem to Bethany near the eastern slopes of the Mount of Olives. He had commanded His disciples to, "Go into all the world and preach the gospel to every creature. He who believes and is baptized will be saved; but he who does not believe will be condemned." He explained that signs and wonders would follow the faithful (Mark 16:15–8) and that "All authority has been given to Me in heaven and earth. Go therefore and make disciples of all the nations, baptizing them in the name of the Father and of the Son and of the Holy Spirit, teaching them to observe all things that I have commanded you; and lo, I am with you even to the end of the age" (Matthew 28:19–20).

He told them to remain in the city to wait for the Promise of the Father that He had told them about. He explained, "For John truly baptized with water, but you shall be baptized with the Holy Spirit not many days from now." They asked Him if this was the time He'd be restoring the kingdom of Israel. Jesus replied, "It is not for you to know the times or seasons which the Father has put in His own authority. But you shall receive power when the Holy Spirit has come upon you; and you shall be witnesses to Me in Jerusalem and in all Judea and Samaria and to the end of the earth."

Mark 16:19–20, Luke 24:50–53, and Acts 1:4–9 reveal that after He spoke, Jesus lifted up His hands and blessed the disciples. While He blessed them, He departed and was carried into heaven on a cloud, where He was seated to the right hand of the Father. Acts 1:10–11 records: "And while they looked steadfastly toward heaven as He went up, behold, two men (angels who appeared as men) stood by them in white apparel, who also said, 'Men of Galilee, why do you stand gazing up into heaven? This same Jesus who was taken up from you into heaven, will so come in like manner as you saw Him go into heaven." They worshiped Jesus and returned with great joy, and remained together as He instructed.

In the words of Luke in Acts 1:3, it's implied that there may have been others who saw Jesus in the forty days He appeared after His crucifixion, speaking of the things pertaining to the Kingdom of God.

Post-Ascension Encounters with Jesus

Acts 9:3–9, 17, along with 1 Corinthians 15:8 and 9:1, record that when the Apostle Paul was on his journey to persecute Christians, on the road to Damascus, Jesus intervened. However, instead of appearing in bodily form as He had before, He appeared in the form of a Great Light and Voice witnessed by many.

Though it is not recorded in the Bible, there are innumerable other individuals who have personally encountered Jesus in the over two thousand years since His resurrection. Each encounter is different, because God relates to each and every one of us individually. I've shared some of my experiences in this book where I've personally encountered Him. And although each time is truly awesome and deeply significant, there is none as precious as that first night when I was home alone in my condominium. That was the night that I found the love I'd always longed for. That was the night that Jesus took my deepest pain and turned it in to joy. My life that night was forever changed, and I am eternally grateful.

The Overwhelming Evidence of Prophecies

According to the conservative estimate of experts, if only forty-eight of the prophecies predicting the birth, life, death, and resurrection of Jesus Christ were fulfilled (scholars estimate He fulfilled over three hundred), the chance would be one in 10^{157}, which is the number 1 with 157 zeros following.[1] Simply considering the statistical probability for only forty-eight fulfilled prophecies is not something I can fully get my mind around, let alone three hundred!

Let me conclude this chapter with one more prophecy. Daniel 9:26 prophesies, "After this period of sixty-two sets of seven, the Anointed One will be killed, appearing to have accomplished nothing, and a ruler will arise whose armies will destroy the city and the Temple" (NLT).

Did this happen? Yes. In AD 70, thirty-nine years after Jesus was killed, a ruler named Titus (who later became Emperor of Rome) led the Roman legions into Jerusalem, where they destroyed the City and the Temple. This completed the messianic prophecy of Daniel 9:24–26 and made it impossible for anyone to appear after the year AD 70 and make a legitimate claim to fulfillment of the messianic prophecies.[2]

History and the Old Testament prophecies are clear: Jesus of Nazareth is the Anointed One, the Messiah, the Holy One of God, and the Lamb of God. As a human being, the most important thing you can do in your life is investigate these claims and build a personal relationship with Jesus.

Chapter Seventeen

Will You Believe?

I was booked to speak for a women's weekend retreat and had arrived early. I enjoy being there when the women arrive, so I can meet and greet them too. We were gathered in a social hall, when from behind me approached a tall, commanding woman. Before ever making eye contact with me, but directing her comment to me, she proclaimed, "I simply can't believe in a God who will send people to eternal hell, just because they don't believe that Jesus was anything other than a good Teacher." Yep, with that you could hear the proverbial pin drop. All pairs of eyes were on me, waiting for my response. I hadn't even established rapport with these women. They hadn't yet heard me speak. I knew my response had to be solid or it would be a very long weekend. I prayed. I opened my mouth and heard myself say, "Well, are you seeking to find the truth, or do you think you've already found it?" A queried look appeared on the woman's face and the chatter in the room resumed. My God-assisted response seemed to satisfy them.

During the weekend, I was able to reveal that God didn't create hell for humanity. It was created for fallen angels—those spirit beings who chose to be enemies of God. God has done everything possible to offer any and every one who wants the opportunity to be reconciled to Him, through faith in Jesus Christ. God offers each one of us escape from this fallen, corrupt world.

Intentional Examination

I revealed at the start of this book that I lived nearly thirty years believing my life was based on truth, only to discover I had been deceived. Deception is the tool the enemy of God used in the Garden of Eden to lure Adam and Eve away from God. It's the same tactic he continues to use to this very day. Unless we intentionally examine what we believe and why we believe it, it's highly possible we are deceived and don't know it. I don't want you to be deceived, and neither does God.

When we examine anything with the intention of arriving at truth, we must apply logic. Logic is the science of correct reasoning through objective truth. For something to be logically correct, it must be objectively true, meaning there is no personal bias involved and each thought proves the other. By using the basic principles of logic, we can identify faulty arguments and reasoning.[1]

Logic is an actual science that follows clearly defined rules and tests for critical thinking. Logic relies on objective, verifiable proof, and through the process of reasoning sound conclusions can be reached. Reasoning without objective, verifiable evidence can produce conclusions that are based on unsubstantiated personal opinion. However, the word "reasoning" also refers to the act of conversing with others in an attempt to influence or change his or her personal opinion.[2]

Using sound logic is what God wants us to do. Isaiah 1:18 reads, "Come now, and let us reason together, says the Lord." God wants us to effectively reason out what we choose to believe.

Considered Faith

With this book, I have sought to (1) define the faith crisis, (2) explain how we've arrived at a crisis of faith, and (3) appeal to your intellect and spirit. I want you to realize the eternal importance of examining what you believe and why you believe it.

Through logic and reason, backed by incredible amounts of objective, verifiable evidence and an honest spiritual desire, I've concluded that the Christian faith provides the best possible explanation of the origin of creation, the existence and nature of God, the reality of pain and suffering, and the conclusion of evil.

Faith is not an obscure concept. Sound faith is based on a sufficient amount of objective, verifiable evidence to allow one to believe what is yet to be proven or that which is not seen. No one wants to live their life on the basis of a lie because our Creator has made us with an innate understanding of moral right and wrong—good and evil. God created us to desire truth, and though living in this fallen world, it is something we must proactively seek.

Knowledge of truth in and of itself is not faith. It is a basis of faith, but it alone is not faith. When Jesus Christ spoke of faith, He used a particular Greek word. That word was *pistis* (4102 in *Strong's Exhaustive Concordance*, page 58 of the Greek Dictionary of the New Testament). It means to persuade, or to be persuaded—more particularly, to be persuaded to come to trust, to have faith. The very purpose of Christ's existence was to persuade people to trust, to have faith in Him as the promised Redeemer, and to have faith in the nature, will, and character of God. All that Jesus said and did was in effort to persuade people to place their faith in Him so that they could be reconciled to God, forever.

Believing Is Only the First Part of Saving Faith

Many people and spirit beings know the truth about Jesus but they choose not to place their faith in Him. James 2:19 reads, "You say you have faith, for you believe that God is One. Good for you! Even the demons believe this, and they tremble in terror" (NLT).

Faith to believe in Jesus as one's personal Savior is a gift from God, and is never something that can be produced by people. In short, *pistis*/faith for the believer is God's divine persuasion, which is quite distinct from human belief or confidence—although human belief and confidence are involved once faith has been bestowed.

Hebrews 11:1 defines *faith* as "the confidence that what we hope for will actually happen; it gives us assurance about things we cannot see" (NLT). Faith is a conviction that we have regarding something that allows us to act utterly assured of the results. This is not natural to man. It is not natural for anyone to act on something as if it exists before it is actually visible.

Romans 10:17 reveals that faith comes by hearing the Word of God. The Word of God is a term that has several meanings. It can mean the written word of God, the Bible, it can mean Jesus, who is referred to in John 1 as God's Word made flesh, and it can mean the spoken Word of God.

Romans 12:3 reveals that it is God who allots a measure of faith to each man. Hebrews 12:2 makes it clear that Jesus is the Author and Perfecter of our faith. Ephesians 28 reveals that it is by grace from God through faith in Jesus that man is restored into a right relationship with God. This is not, by any measure, something we do or can do. Faith, by God's grace, is a gift from God.

Grace, as it is used in the Bible, means "the divine influence upon the human heart, and its reflection in the life (5485 in *Strong's*

Exhaustive Concordance, page 77 of the Greek Dictionary of the New Testament). It's a God-given benefit, favor, or gift available to all mankind.

John 3:16 summarizes, "For God loved the world so much that He gave His one and only Son, so that everyone who believes in him will not perish, but have eternal life" (NLT).

Receiving Is the Second Part of Saving Faith

God births faith into the willing heart—a heart that's been softened through hearing the Word of God. When that person believes Jesus is who He claimed to be and acts on their God-persuaded faith, that person is redeemed. He or she is pardoned, and the punishment for sin he or she deserved is declared paid in full by the life, death, and resurrection of Jesus. Anyone who is willing to *believe and receive* Jesus by faith is assured salvation. Saving faith is simple and certain.

Beyond the initial act of believing faith, Christians can enjoy a sustaining faith. God continuously births faith in the yielded believer so he or she can know what He prefers—that is, to know the persuasion of His will. First John 5:4 reads: "For every child of God defeats this evil world, and we achieve this victory through our faith" (NLT).

Pistis/faith, in secular antiquity, referred to a guarantee (warranty). In scripture, faith is God's warranty certifying that the revelation He established will come to pass His way. *Pistis*/faith is also used collectively—of all the times God has revealed His will, which includes the full revelation of scripture. Indeed, God guarantees that all of this revelation will come to pass![3]

Numbers 23:19 reads, "God is not a man, so he does not lie. He is not human, so He does not change his mind. Has He ever spoken and failed to act? Has He ever promised and not carried it through?"(NLT).

Isaiah 55:11 affirms this: "It is the same with my word. I send it out, and it always produces fruit. It will accomplish all I want it to, and it will prosper everywhere I send it" (NLT).

Ezekiel 12:25 assures us, "For I am the LORD! If I say it, it will happen. There will be no more delays, you rebels of Israel. I will fulfill my threat of destruction in your own lifetime. I, the Sovereign LORD, have spoken!" (NLT).

Matthew 5:18 confirms again, "I tell you the truth, until heaven and earth disappear, not even the smallest detail of God's law will disappear until its purpose is achieved" (NLT).

Second Timothy 3:16 holds up Scripture as the standard we need, "All Scripture is inspired by God and is useful to teach us what is true and to make us realize what is wrong in our lives. It corrects us when we are wrong and teaches us to do what is right" (NLT).

Redeeming Faith

Faith that pleases God must be first pure and undefiled. Attempting to "mix faiths" not only corrupts what faith a person does have; it displeases God and renders the effectiveness of the faith impotent. The faith Jesus died to provide for us is nothing less than the enabling power of God in and through believers to personally overcome sin.

If you believe and if you desire, God will birth faith in you. If by believing-faith you declare that you want to receive Jesus as your personal Savior and Lord, it shall be done for you. You have the promise of God in 1 John 5:14: "Now this is the confidence that we have in Him, that if we ask anything according to His will, He hears us. And if we know that He hears us, whatever we ask, we know that we have the petitions that we have asked of Him."

From the beginning of time, God has revealed that it is His will that anyone who desires can be restored unto Him. However, Jesus cautioned His followers, asking them to consider the cost before making a commitment of faith to Him. Christianity and all it stands for is not welcomed by the world. I ask you with a true heart of compassion: wouldn't you rather be welcomed by God?

The Bible is clear that the greatest unpardonable sin is unbelief. With all that God has already done to reveal truth, with the price He has already personally paid to secure your redemption unto Himself, it's understandable that unbelief would be the highest insult to God.

Hebrews 11:6 states, "And it is impossible to please God without faith. Anyone who wants to come to Him must believe that God exists and that He rewards those who sincerely seek Him" (NLT).

God offers anyone who wants to be united with Him the promise of a renewed and Everlasting Life: "For God loved the world so much that He gave His one and only Son, so that everyone who believes in Him will not perish but have eternal life. God sent His Son into the world not to judge the world, but to save the world through Him. There is no judgment against anyone who believes in Him. But anyone who does not believe in Him has already been judged for not believing in God's one and only Son" (NLT). This quote is from John 3:16–18, and are the very words of Jesus.

If you believe and you now want Jesus to be your personal Savior, to save you not only from an eternal hell, but from the ravages of sin in this life, you simply need to pray to God declaring faith in Jesus as your personal Savior and Lord of your life.

According to God's Word in Romans 10:9, "If you confess with your mouth the Lord Jesus, and believe in your heart that God has raised Him from the dead, you will be saved." Will you believe?

If you want the eternal peace and assurance Christ offers, you simply need to pray something like the following: "God in heaven, I acknowledge You as the Creator of all that exists, as the Father of all living. I better understand that in Your perfect Trinity, You offer a plan for each human being to be restored to You. I want to be redeemed. I want to be restored into a right relationship with You. So I willingly confess that Jesus is the Promised Redeemer. By faith I declare He was God in human flesh, who defeated sin in my behalf, by the power of Your Holy Spirit. I receive Him as my personal Savior and Lord, claiming Your promise by faith, that through Him, I am now restored in right relationship with You forever and ever. Amen."

It is my prayer that this book will bring gentle and loving conviction by the Holy Spirit through the experience of God's grace and guidance to make certain your faith is pure. Only then can you confidently move forward in this world, able to overcome any adversity that comes your way. No one ever raises their hand when I ask, "Who in this room wants to live your life on the basis of a lie?" With this book, you have been presented truth.

Chapter Endnotes

Chapter Two

1. Dan Harris, "Americans Surprisingly Flexible about Religion and Faith," *ABC News with Diane Sawyer* (December 2009), http://abcnews.go.com/WN/pew-studyfinds-americans-surprisingly-flexible-faith-religion/story?id=9306080.

2. "Many Americans Mix Multiple Faiths," *Pew Research Center's Forum on Religion and Public Life* (December 2009), http://www.pewforum.org/Other-Beliefs-and-Practices/Many-Americans-Mix-Multiple-Faiths.aspx.

3. "Survey: More Americans Mix-Match Religions," *Faith on NBC News* (December 2009), http://www.msnbc.msn.com/id/34352940/ns/us_newsfaith/t/survey-more-americans-mix-match-religions.

4. Eric Gorski, "Survey: Americans Mix and Match Faiths," *Orange Counter Register* (December 2009), http://www.ocregister.com/news/americans-54393-ocprint-say-attend.html.

5. David Barton, "Deconstructionism and the Left," *Wall Builders* (July 28, 2011), http://www.wallbuilders.com/libissuesarticles.asp?id=95644.

6. Erwin W. Lutzer, *Christ Among Other gods: A Defense of Christ in an Age of Tolerance* (Chicago: Moody Publishers, 1994), 12.

7. George Barna, *Absolute Confusion* (Ventura, CA: Gospel Light/Regal Books, 1993), 15.

8. J. P. Moreland, "'Choosin' My Religion': J. P. Moreland Shows How to Make a Nonarbitrary Choice about One's Religion," *Focus on the Family* (April 23, 2013), http://www.focusonthefamily.com/faith/christian_worldview/why_is_a_christian_worldview_important/choosin_my_religion.aspx.

9. Lutzer, *Christ Among Other gods*, 22.

10. Francis Collins, "Learning the Language of God," in *Test of FAITH: Spiritual Journeys with Scientists*, ed. Ruth Bancewiz (Eugene, OR: Wipf and Stock Publishers), 1–9.

Chapter Three

1. "Emotional Management Scale," from Emotional Intelligence Evaluation, *Psychtests Profile* (April 23, 2013), http://testyourself.psychtests.com.

2. M. Q. Jeffrey, "Intelligence (IQ) vs. Emotional Intelligence (EQ)," *Hub Pages* (April 23, 2013), http://mqjeffrey.hubpages.com/hub/Intelligence-IQ-vs-Emotional-Intelligence-EQ.

3. "Is Truth Objective or Subjective?" *Truthnet*, no. 2 (April 23, 2013), http://www.truthnet.org/Christianity/Apologetics/Truth2.

4. Ibid.

5. Lutzer, *Christ Among Other gods*, 53.

6. "Is Truth Objective or Subjective?" *Truthnet*, no. 2 (April 23, 2013), http://www.truthnet.org/Christianity/Apologetics/Truth2.

Chapter Four

1. "What Is Religious Pluralism?" *Pluralism Project* (April 23, 2013), http://pluralism.org/pages/pluralism/what_is_pluralism.

2. Lutzer, *Christ Among Other gods*, 13–14.

3. Alan Shlemon, "So Many Bad Arguments against Religion, So Little Time," *Stand to Reason* (September 2005), http://www.str.org/site/DocServer/alanshlemonnews0509.pdf?docID=404.

4. Ibid.

5. "The Big Religion Comparison Chart," *Religion Facts* (April 23, 2013), http://www.religionfacts.com/big_religion_chart.htm.

6. "World POPClock Projection," *US Census Bureau* (February 2008), http://www.census.gov/population/popclockworld.html.

7. *Wikipedia*, s.v. "God in Islam," and "Islam," last modified March 2012, http://en.wikipedia.org/wiki/God_in_Islam and http://en.wikipedia.org/wiki/Islam.

8. "Humanist Manifesto III," *American Humanist Association* (April 25, 2013), http://www.americanhumanist.org/Humanism/Humanist_Manifesto_III.

9. Ariela Pelaia, "What Do Jews Believe?" About.com Guide (April 23, 2013), http://judaism.about.com/od/judaismbasics/a/whatdojewsbelieve.htm; "Jewish Beliefs," *Jewish Beliefs* (April 23, 2013), http://www.jewishbeliefs.org; *Wikipedia*, s.v. "God in Judaism," last modified March 2012, http://en.wikipedia.org/wiki/God_in_Judaism; John Piper (2009), "Did Old Testament Jews

Believe in a Triune God?" (video), *YouTube*, http://www.youtube.com/watch?v=wL1Ac4HICZw.

10. Lutzer, *Christ Among Other gods*, 29.

Chapter Five

1. "Religion Library: Judaism." *Patheos Library* (April 23, 2013), http://www.patheos.com/Library/Judaism.html.

2. Nissan Mindel, "Abraham's Early Life," *Chabad-Lubavitch Media Center* (April 23, 2013), http://www.chabad.org/library/article_cdo/aid/112063/jewish/Abrahams-Early-Life.htm.

3. Ralph F. Wilson, "Abraham: An Introduction to His Life and Times," *Jesus Walk* (April 23, 2103), http://www.jesuswalk.com/abraham/0_intro.htm.

4. John Dickson, *A Spectator's Guide to World Religions: An Introduction to the Big Five,* (Oxford: Lion Hudson PLC, 2008), 91

5. "Ask Rabbi Simmons: Abraham Breaking Idols," *About.com* (April 23, 2013) http://judaism.about.com/library/3_askrabbi_o/bl_simmons_abrahamidols.htm.

6. Mike Shreve, *In Search of the True Light* (Cleveland: Deeper Revelation Books, 2006), 73–74.

7. "Timelines and Chronology," *Teaching Hearts* (April 23, 2013), http://www.teachinghearts.org/dre00timeline.html; Matthew McGee, "Old Testament Timeline," (April 23, 2013), http://www.matthewmcgee.org/ottimlin.html.

8. Rabbi Mordechai Becher, "The Ten Plagues—Live from Egypt," *Ohr Somayach International* (April 23, 2013), http://ohr.edu/838.

9. Dennis Bratcher, "The Date of the Exodus," *Christian Research Institute's Voice* (April 23, 2013), http://www.cresourcei.org/exodusdate.html; "The Exodus and Ancient Egyptian Records," *Jewish Action* (Spring 1995), http://www.starways.net/lisa/essays/exodus.html; Brad Aaronson, "When Was the Exodus?" *Orthodox Union* (April 23, 2013), http://www.ou.org/chagim/pesach/whenex.htm.

10. "Character Study of King David," *Thompson Chain-Reference Study Bible*, ed. Frank Charles Thompson, New King James version (Thomas Nelson, Inc., 1982), 2107–2108; "Judaism," *The Patheos Library* (April 23, 2013), http://www.patheos.com/Library/Judaism.html.

11. "Why Study History of Judaism," *Simple to Remember* (April 23, 2013), http://www.simpletoremember.com/articles/a/study-jewish-history/

12. Huston Smith, *The World's Religions: Our Great Wisdom Traditions* (New York: Harper Collins, 1991), 272.

13. Ibid., 273.

14. Ibid., 274.

Chapter Six

1. Ryuei Michael McCormick, "The Path of the World Honored One," *Nichiren's Coffee House* (April 25, 2013), http://nichirenscoffeehouse.net/Ryuei/LifeofBuddha.html.

2. Huston Smith, *The World's Religions: Our Great Wisdom Traditions* (New York: Harper Collins, 1991), 85.

3. Ibid., 85–86.

4. Ibid., 86.

5. Ibid., 86–87.

6. Ibid., 89.

7. Ibid., 91–92.

8. John Dickson, *A Spectator's Guide to World Religions: An Introduction to the Big Five* (Oxford: Lion Hudson PLC, 2008), 69–70.

9. Ibid., 71–75.

10. Ryuei Michael McCormick, "Buddhism in America," *Nichiren's Coffee House* (April 25, 2013), http://nichirenscoffeehouse.net/Ryuei/Buddhism-in-America.html.

11. John Dickson, *A Spectator's Guide to World Religions: An Introduction to the Big Five* (Oxford: Lion Hudson PLC, 2008), 81.

12. "The Story of Buddha-3," Wit and Wisdom (blog), August 2008, http://witandwisdom4u.blogspot.com/2012/08/the-story-of-budha-3.html#!/2012/08/the-story-of-budha-3.html.

13. Radhika Abeysekera, "The Appeal of Buddhism in the West," *Buddah Sasana* (April 25, 2013), http://www.budsas.org/ebud/ebdha276.htm.

Chapter Seven

1. "Hinduism," *Religious Facts* (April 25, 2013), http://www.religionfacts.com/hinduism/index.htm.

2. Huston Smith, *The World's Religions: Our Great Wisdom Traditions* (New York: Harper Collins, 1991), 63–64.

3. "Hinduism vs. Christianity," *Scribd* (April 25, 2013), http://www.scribd.com/doc/6722833/Hinduism-vs-Christianity.

4. "Popularity of Hinduism, Related Teachings Rises in U.S. Faith: More than 1 Million Devotees Live Here, but Many Millions More Use Such Elements as Yoga and Meditation," *L.A. Times* (August 12, 1995), http://articles.latimes.com/1995-08-12/local/me-34401_1_hinduism-today.

5. "Hinduism vs. Christianity," *Scribd* (April 25, 2013), http://www.scribd.com/doc/6722833/Hinduism-vs-Christianity

6. "Popularity of Hinduism, Related Teachings Rises in U.S. Faith: More than 1 Million Devotees Live Here, but Many Millions More Use Such Elements as Yoga and Meditation," *L.A. Times* (August 12, 1995), http://articles.latimes.com/1995-08-12/local/me-34401_1_hinduism-today.

7. Ibid.

8. "Overview of Hinduism," Religion Facts website (April 25, 2013), http://www.religionfacts.com/hinduism/overview.htm.

Chapter Eight

1. Warren Smith, "Oprah and Friends to Teach Course on New Age Christ," *Kjos Ministries* (November 2007), http://www.crossroad.to/articles2/007/smith-oprah.htm.

2. "Oprah and the New Age Christ," *Snopes.com* (April 25, 2013), http://www.snopes.com/politics/religion/newageoprah.asp.

3. Warren Smith, "Oprah and Friends to Teach Course on New Age Christ," *Kjos Ministries* (November 2007), http://www.crossroad.to/articles2/007/smith-oprah.htm.

4. Ibid.

5. "A Secular Humanist Declaration," *Council for Secular Humanism* (April 25, 2013), http://www.secularhumanism.org/index.php

6. "Beyond Atheism, Beyond Agnosticism, Secular Humanism," and

"What Are the Secular Humanist Values," *Council for Secular Humanism* (April 25, 2013), http://www.secularhumanism.org.

7. "A Secular Humanist Declaration," *Council for Secular Humanism* (April 25, 2013), http://www.secularhumanism.org/index.php?section=main&page=declaration.

8. Ibid.

9. Ibid.

10. Ibid.

Chapter Nine

1. "What Is the Koran?" *Atlantic Monthly* 283, no. 1. 43–56. Also available at (May 7, 2013) http://www.theatlantic.com/past/docs/issues/99jan/koran2.htm.

2. Huston Smith, *The World's Religions: Our Great Wisdom Traditions* (New York: Harper Collins, 1991), 223–224.

3. John Dickson, *A Spectator's Guide to World Religions: An Introduction to the Big Five* (Oxford: Lion Hudson PLC, 2008), 177.

4. Huston Smith, *The World's Religions: Our Great Wisdom Traditions* (New York: Harper Collins, 1991), 230.

5. Ibid., 222, 230.

6. Ibid., 230.

7. John Dickson, *A Spectator's Guide to World Religions: An Introduction to the Big Five* (Oxford: Lion Hudson PLC, 2008), 187–189.

8. "Earlier Muslims Say Much More of the Koran Was Lost," Islam Forum, *Topix* (April 25, 2013), http://www.topix.com/forum/religion/islam/TI9I7ROTLS78D84C8.

9. "Background of Islam," *Xenos Christian Fellowship* (April 25, 2013), http://www.xenos.org/essays/islam.htm.

10. Ibid.

11. "Question and Answer: Muslim View of Jesus' Crucifixion," *Orthodox Presbyterian Church* (April 25, 2013), http://www.opc.org/qa.html?question_id=52.

12. Imam Mohamed Baianonie, "The Islamic View of the Human Being" (July 4, 1997), http://islam1.org./khutub/View_of_Human_Being.htm.

13. Mark Hartwig, "Spread by the Sword?" *Answering Islam* (April 25, 2013), http://www.answering-islam.org/Terrorism/by_the_sword.html.

14. F.A. Klein, *The Religion of Islam* (London: K. Paul, Trench, Trübner, 1906), 174–175.

15. "Contemporary Islamist Ideology Authorizing Genocide Murder," *Middle East Media Research Institute* (April 25, 2013), http://www.memri.org/report/en/0/0/0/0/0/0/1049.htm.

Chapter Ten

1. Hank Hanegraaff, "M-A-P-S to Guide You through Biblical Reliability," *Christian Research Institute*, article DB-011, June 1993.

2. Elesha Coffman, "Why Are the Protestant and Catholic Bibles Different?" *Christianity Today* (April 25, 2013), http://www.christianitytoday.com/ch/asktheexpert/jun01.html.

3. "Westminster Shorter Catechism," *Westminster Shorter Catechism*, question 10 (April 25, 2013), http://www.reformed.org/documents/WSC.html.

4. *Thompson Chain-Reference Study Bible*, ed. Frank Charles Thompson, New King James version (Thomas Nelson, Inc., 1982), 4.

5. Ibid., Gen. 3:14–15, 4.

6. Ibid., Gen. 3:16, 4.

7. Ibid., Gen. 3:17–19, 4.

8. Ibid., Gen. 17:20–21, Gen. 21:18–21, 19, 24.

9. Arthur C. Custance, "The Genealogy from Adam to Jesus Christ," *Lambert Dophin* (April 25, 2013), http://www.ldolphin.org/2adams.html.

10. *Thompson Chain-Reference Study Bible*, ed. Frank Charles Thompson, New King James version (Thomas Nelson, Inc., 1982), 1497, 1499, 1516.

Chapter Eleven

1. Huston Smith, *The World's Religions: Our Great Wisdom Traditions* (New York: Harper Collins, 1991), 3.

2. *Spirit Battle for Souls* (April 25, 2013), www.spiritbattleforsouls.org.

3. Eugene Peterson, *The Message: The Bible in Contemporary Language,* Luke 14:25–33 (Colorado Springs: NavPress, 2002), 1889–1890.

Chapter Twelve

1. "Is the World in a Conflict between Good and Evil?" Forum, *Being Jewish* (April 25, 2013), http://www.beingjewish.com/faqs/conflict.html; "Does Judaism Believe in Satan?" Forum, *Being Jewish* (April 25, 2013), http://www.beingjewish.com/basics/satan.html; "The Nature of G-d," *Judaism 101* (April 25, 2013), http://www.jewfaq.org/g-d.htm.

2. Sherman A. Jackson, "The Problem of Suffering: Muslim Theological Reflections," *Huffington Post* (September 2010), http://www.huffingtonpost.com/sherman-a-jackson/on-godand-suffering-musl_b_713994.html; "What Does Islam Believe about the End?"

Islam and World Events (April 25, 2013), http://www.truthnet.org/islam/Islam-Bible/4Islambeliefs/index.htm.

3. Dan Story, *Defending Your Faith: Reliable Answers for a New Generation of Seekers and Skeptics* (Grand Rapids, MI: Kregel Publications, 1997), 167.

4. Ibid., 169.

5. *Thompson Chain-Reference Study Bible*, ed. Frank Charles Thompson, New King James version (Thomas Nelson, 1982), 4.

6. Angelo Caiazzo, "Tales of Human Origins: The East to China and Buddhism," *Truthopia* (blog), January 2010, http://truthopia.wordpress.com/2010/01/16.

7. "Hinduism," *True Light* (April 25, 2013), http://www.thetruelight.net/religions/hinduism.htm.

8. *Wikipedia*, s.v. "New Age," last modified on April 25, 2013, http://en.wikipedia.org/wiki/New_Age.

9. Dan Story, *Defending Your Faith: Reliable Answers for a New Generation of Seekers and Skeptics* (Grand Rapids, MI: Kregel Publications, 1997), 170–172.

10. *Thompson Chain-Reference Study Bible*, ed. Frank Charles Thompson, New King James version (Thomas Nelson, Inc., 1982), 4.

11. Ibid., Gen. 3:16, 4.

12. Ibid., Gen. 3:17–19, 4.

13. Dan Story, *Defending Your Faith: Reliable Answers for a New Generation of Seekers and Skeptics* (Grand Rapids, MI: Kregel Publications, 1997), 176.

Chapter Thirteen

1. John Dickson, *A Spectator's Guide to World Religions: An Introduction to the Big Five* (Oxford: Lion Hudson PLC, 2008), 213.

2. "Islam vs. Christianity: What Are the Major Differences?" All About God Ministries, ed. M. Houdmann, P. Matthrews-Rose, and R. Miles (2002–2012), http://www.allaboutreligion.org/islam-vs-christianity-faq.htm.

3. John Dickson, *A Spectator's Guide to World Religions: An Introduction to the Big Five* (Oxford: Lion Hudson PLC, 2008), 214.

4. "Islam vs. Christianity: What Are the Major Differences?" All About God Ministries, ed. M. Houdmann, P. Matthrews-Rose, and R. Miles (2002–2012), http://www.allaboutreligion.org/islam-vs-christianity-faq.htm.

5. John Dickson, *A Spectator's Guide to World Religions: An Introduction to the Big Five* (Oxford: Lion Hudson PLC, 2008), 211–212.

6. Ibid., 210–211.

7. Warren Smith, "Oprah and Friends to Teach Course on New Age Christ," Kjos Ministries (November 2007), http://www.crossroad.to/articles2/007/smith-oprah.htm.

8. *Jewish Encyclopedia*, s.v. "Josephus, Flavius," (May 7, 2013), http://www.jewishencyclopedia.com/articles/8905-josephus-flavius.

9. Matt Slick, "Regarding the Quotes from the Historian Josephus about Jesus," Christian Apologetics and Research Ministry (April 25, 2013), http://carm.org/regarding-quotes-historian-josephus-about-jesus.

10. "Non-Biblical Accounts about New Testament Events and/or People," Christian Apologetics and Research Ministry (April 25, 2013), http://carm.org/non-Biblical-accounts-new-testament-events-andor-people.

11. N. S. Gill, "Tacitus the Roman Historian," About.com (April 25, 2013), http://ancienthistory.about.com/od/historianstacitus/a/Tacitus.htm.

12. Alfred John Church and William Jackson Brodribb, "The Works of Tacitus," Sacred Texts (1864–1877), http://www.sacredtexts.com/cla/tac/index.htm.

13. Jona Lendering, "Pliny the Younger (1)," Livius (April 25, 2013), http://www.livius.org/pi-pm/pliny/pliny_y.htm.

14. "Non-Biblical Accounts about New Testament Events and/or People," Christian Apologetics and Research Ministry (April 25, 2013), http://carm.org/non-Biblical-accounts-new-testament-events-andor-people.

15. Ibid.

16. *Encyclopedia Britannica*, s.v. "Lucian," (April 25, 2013), http://www.britannica.com/EBchecked/topic/350566/Lucian.

17. "Non-Biblical Accounts about New Testament Events and/or People," Christian Apologetics and Research Ministry (April 25, 2013), http://carm.org/non-Biblical-accounts-new-testament-events-andor-people.

18. Lutzer, *Christ Among Other gods*, 134.

Chapter Fourteen

1. *Thompson Chain-Reference Study Bible*, ed. Frank Charles Thompson, New King James version (Thomas Nelson, Inc., 1982), 1327–1328.

2. Lutzer, *Christ Among Other gods*, 64–65.

3. *Thompson Chain-Reference Study Bible*, ed. Frank Charles Thompson, New King James version (Thomas Nelson, Inc., 1982), 1322.

4. Ibid., Heb. 4:15, 1558.

5. Ibid., Micah 5:2, 1199.

6. Nick Strobel, "The Star of Bethlehem: An Astronomical Perspective," *Astronomy Notes* (April 25, 2013), http://www.astronomynotes.com/history/bethlehem-star.html.

7. *Thompson Chain-Reference Study Bible*, ed. Frank Charles Thompson, New King James version (Thomas Nelson, Inc., 1982), 1324–1325.

8. Britt Gillette, "Prophecy: The Messiah Will Appear in Jerusalem in A.D. 31," *Britt Gillette* (blog), February 24, 2007, http://brittgillette.com/WordPress/?p=22.

9. "Calendar Conversion Tool," *Abdicate* (April 25, 2013), http://www.abdicate.net/cal.aspx.

10. Britt Gillette, "Prophecy: The Messiah Will Appear in Jerusalem in A.D. 31," *Britt Gillette* (blog), February 24, 2007, http://brittgillette.com/WordPress/?p=22.

11. Ibid.; Mary Fairchild, "Prophecies Jesus Fulfilled," *About.com* (April 25, 2013), http://christianity.about.com/od/Biblefactsandlists/a/Prophecies-Jesus.htm.

Chapter Fifteen

1. *Thompson Chain-Reference Study Bible*, ed. Frank Charles Thompson, New King James version (Thomas Nelson, Inc., 1982), 1374.

2. Ibid., Matt. 3:13–17, 1244

3. Ibid., Matt. 12:39, 1258

4. Ibid., Luke 23:13, 1368

5. Chuck Bumgardner, "The Thickness of the Veil of the Temple," *Orchard Keeper* (April 2010), http://cbumgardner.wordpress.com/2010/04/06/the-thickness-ofthe-temple-veil.

6. Robert L. Plummer, "Something Awry in the Temple? The Rending of the Temple Veil and Early Jewish Sources that Report Unusual Phenomena in the Temple around AD 30," *ETSJETS* (June 2005), http://www.etsjets.org/files/JETS-PDFs/48/48-2/48-2-pp301-316_JETS.pdf; William F. Dakenbring, "Mysterious Events in the Year 30 AD!" *Ensign Message* (June 2004), http://www.ensignmessage.com/archives/mysteriousevents.html; "What Was the Significance of the Veil Being Torn in Two When Jesus Died?" *GotQuestions.org* (April 25, 2013), http://www.gotquestions.org/temple-veil-torn.html.

Chapter Sixteen

1. John Funk, "Statistics and Probability," *Rapture Ready* (April 25, 2013), www.raptureready.com/featured/funk/statistics-probability.html.
2. Britt Gillette, "Messianic Prophecies Fulfilled by Jesus," *Britt Gillette* (blog), (April 25, 2013), http://brittgillette.com/WordPress/?page_id=21.

Chapter Seventeen

1. J. Spindel, "Logic and Reason," *Helium* (April 25, 2013), http://www.helium.com/items/2104105-logic-and-reason.
2. Vanessa Harvey, "What Is the Difference between Logic and Reason?" *Wise Geek* (April 25, 2013), www.wisegeek.com/what-is-the-difference-between-logic-and-reason.htm.
3. Garry Hill, "The Helps Discovery Bible New Testament," *Strong's Exhaustive Concordance*, ref. no. 4102 (April 25, 2013), www.helpsBible.com.

About the Author

Pamela Christian's ministry began in the early 1990s as Teaching Director for Community Bible Study, an independent, international organization. This was followed by invitations to speak across the country for various organizations, which she continues to enjoy with great enthusiasm to this day. Her initial writing work included the development of workbooks for her retreats and conferences. This soon expanded to publication in book compilations, magazines, and several e-books.

Her speaking and writing career translated perfectly into other media, including hosting talk shows on Christian radio, television, and voice-over work. With a certificate in apologetics from Biola University, her passion is to help others in matters of faith, which dubbed her "the Faith Doctor with Your Rx for Life!" Her favorite pastimes are food, family, and friends.

Pam and her husband live in Orange County, CA, with their two grown children living nearby. To book Pam to speak or to learn more, visit www.pamelachristianministries.com.

Examine Your Faith!
Finding Truth in a World of Lies

is the first in a three-book series!

Next is:

Renew Your Hope!
Remedy for Personal Breakthroughs

Last is:

Revive Your Life!
Rest for Your Anxious Heart

To be sure you don't miss the release of all Pam's books, sign up for her monthly EZine!

www.pamelachristianministries.com
Pamela Christian Ministries
18032 Lemon Dr. #C206, Yorba Linda, CA 92886
info@pamelachristianministries.com

CPSIA information can be obtained at www.ICGtesting.com
Printed in the USA
LVOW06s0433270813

349673LV00001B/6/P